Beginner's Guide to Beadweaving

by Diana Rehfield

Published by Diana Rehfield

Copyright © 2017 by Diana Rehfield

All rights reserved.

Second Edition

ISBN-13: 978-1545107584

ISBN-10: 1545107580

Contents

Introduction

Beadweaving is the process of connecting beads together using a needle and thread. Using this technique, you can make very simple to very complex pieces.

Table of Contents

Beadweaving Stitches

There are many beadweaving stitches, including a few primary stitches, and many variants upon those primary stitches (for example, tubular variants).

Here are some of the most common beadweaving stitches.

Stitch Name	Example	Properties
Peyote		The rows are offset. That is, there are "up" rows and "down" rows.
Square		The rows are straight across. This is the same appearance achieved by looming.

Stitch Name	Example	Properties
Herringbone		Beads are added two at a time and each pair of beads slants inward slightly. The first row (top) of the pictured piece is ladder stitch, which is how herringbone stitch is started. Notice that the holes of the beads are facing up and down, as contrasted with the holes in peyote and square stitch, which are pointing side to side.
Right Angle Weave (RAW)		Beads are added in a circular path and the effect is that the beads end up at right angles to each other.
Netting		Beads are added several at a time, going through anchor beads at regular intervals. The anchor beads are gold in this photo.
Brick		The look of brick stitch is similar to peyote but it is worked in a different direction. Brick stitch is excellent for shaped beadwork because it is easy to follow a pattern and make increases and decreases.
Spiral		Spiral stitch creates a rope and can be beaded in a number of ways, including peyote and herringbone. This sample shown is basic spiral stitch with a gold bead core.

Bead Types

There are many different bead types. Seed beads are the most commonly used bead type for beadweaving. They are called *seed beads* because of their small size (like seeds). Seed bead sizes were originally named for the approximate number of beads per inch. 6/0 seed beads were about 6 beads per inch (large) and 15/0 seed beads were about 15 beads per inch (small). The most commonly used seed bead size is 11/0. We will be using size 8/0 seed beads for most of our projects because they are easy to handle and make learning easier. Amounts of seed beads are usually measured in grams when you buy them.

Among seed beads, there are variations. One variation is cylinder versus round. Cylinder beads have a large hole relative to their size and they have walls that are straight up and down and all one width. Common cylinder beads are Miyuki Delica and Toho Treasures. Miyuki and Toho also make round (and other type) beads.

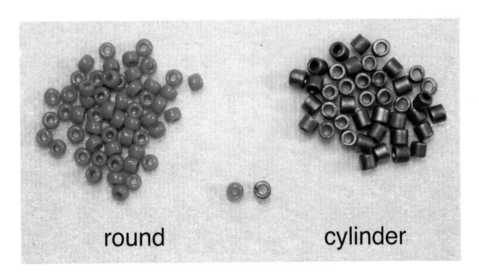

round   cylinder

Bead Finishes

There are many wonderful bead finishes available. Some beads combine finishes, such as transparent matte. Using beads with different finishes in a project provides contrast and interest. Thank you to Terri Ann Fox at foxdenbeads.com for allowing me to use her photos.

Bead Finish	Description	Photo
Opaque	All one color. No additional finish.	

Bead Finish	Description	Photo
Transparent	All one color. Can see through when held up to the light.	
Matte or Frosted	All one color, can be opaque or transparent. Looks like a sanded finish, not shiny.	
Silver-Lined	Transparent with a silver (or other color) lining inside the bead.	
Metallic or Galvanized	Metallic coating on the outside of the bead.	
AB (Aurora Borealis) or Rainbow	A coating added to the outside of the bead that reflects different shades of light.	

Thread Types

As with seed beads, there are many types of thread. I recommend a bonded thread called FireLine (gel-spun polyethylene, 0.15mm diameter) 6lb test for most projects. It is a good general-purpose thread, even though it was originally fishing line. For larger beads (for example 6/0), you might want to use heavier FireLine, such as 8lb or 10lb. For very small beads, such as 15/0 beads, you might want to use 4lb FireLine.

FireLine is not good for projects that require a soft feel, such as fringe. For those projects, you can use a nylon thread such as Nymo, Silamide, K-O, S-Lon, or One-G.

Clasps

A *clasp* is the device you will use to keep your bracelet, necklace, or anklet closed while wearing it. Here are some common clasp types.

Clasp Type	Description	Photo
Toggle	Toggle clasps consist of a loop and a bar. They are easy to attach and easy for the wearer to use if attached properly.	
Lobster Claw	Lobster claw clasps do indeed resemble the claw of a lobster. They are spring-loaded and close around a ring on the other end of the item. They are easy to attach but can be difficult for some wearers to use.	
Magnetic	Magnetic clasps consist of two parts, with a magnet on each part. They are easy to attach and very easy for the wearer to use. However, you should attach a safety chain when you use these clasps so the wearer does not lose the item if the magnets come apart.	
Slide Lock	Slide lock clasps consist of two parts, each of which has a tube. One tube is smaller than the other so it can slide into the larger tube. Slide lock clasps take a bit more effort to attach to the item but they provide a clean look and are generally easy for the wearer to put on. Here are guidelines for choosing slide lock clasp width for use with Delica beads: - 16 columns: 3-loop - 20 columns: 4-loop - 24 columns: 5-loop - 28 columns: 6-loop	

Clasp Type	Description	Photo
Button	Button and loop clasps can add a very nice design element to your bracelet. The button can be attached on the bracelet or on the end. The loop is usually beaded. They are easy to create and generally easy for the wearer to put on.	Work and photo from Sharon Deuel Gies

Tools

I recommend the following tools for beadweaving.

Tool Name	Description	Photo
Beading mat	A beading mat provides a work surface that helps keeps your beads from rolling away from you.	
Needles	Beading needles are commonly 2 inches long and come in a variety of widths. I recommend using Size 10 beading needles for most projects.	John James Est. 1840 Beading Aiguilles à Perles Aufreinadeln L4320 010 25 Needles
Thread	You can use any type of sturdy thread. I recommend Crystal FireLine 6lb fishing line, which can be purchased from sporting goods stores and many craft stores. FireLine is very strong and does not fray in most situations.	FireLine
Cutting tool	FireLine can be difficult to cut. Oddly enough, child scissors (like Fiskars) work really well. I use Xuron 440 High Precision Scissors and they have just started to lose their edge after several years of use. A thread burner can also be used for cutting threads and tidying up thread ends.	

Tool Name	Description	Photo
Magnifying glasses	If you are lucky and have perfect vision, you won't need these. But for most people they are helpful. I use 2.75 magnification and you should use whatever works best for you.	
Light source	You definitely need good light for beading. I use full-spectrum lights because they help me see the bead colors most effectively. Many people use an Ott lamp because it provides bright light in a neutral color.	
Ruler	A ruler with both inches and millimeters is very helpful since many beads and findings are measured in millimeters.	
Tape	Many beaders use what is called a *stop bead* to keep their beads from coming off the thread at the beginning of a project. I prefer a piece of tape and will describe that technique in the Peyote tutorial.	
Flat nose pliers	Recommended but not necessary for flattening the end of FireLine to make it easier to thread onto a needle.	

Tool Name	Description	Photo
Bead scoop	Like the scoop waiters use to remove crumbs from your table, a bead scoop allows you to move beads easily on your mat.	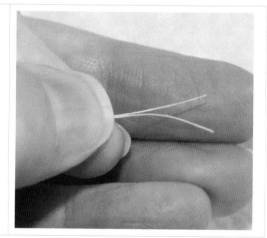

Adding Thread

There are a number of methods for adding thread during a project. I will show the method I use for adding thread in the following situations:

- When I'm using 11/0 or smaller beads.
- When it would be difficult to get a knot through the beads, such as in brick stitch.

If I am using larger beads or doing square stitch projects, I use the square knot/melted thread end method. This allows you to pull the threads so you just end up with a small "blob" join. There are a number of video tutorials that show how to do this and I recommend them since they are easier to follow than a photo tutorial for this technique. One of my favorite videos of this technique is by one of my favorite beaders, Patrick Duggan. Search for "FireLine join" in youtube to find the videos. The square knot/melted end method only works for thread that melts into a blob on the end, such as FireLine. If you are using a thread that does not melt on the end, use the technique described below.

1. Pick a location near but not at the beginning of a row, so the knot will be hidden in the beading and will not show on the edge.
2. Pull a length of thread to match the length between your outstretched arms and cut from the spool.
3. Line up the end of the new thread with the end of the old thread.

4. At the thread ends by your beadwork, make a loop of the two lengths of thread.

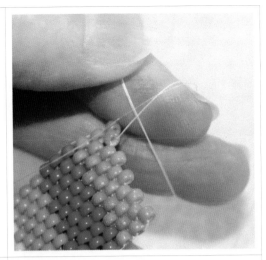

5. Pull the loose ends through the loop.

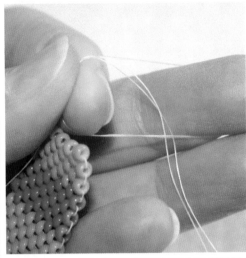

6. Work the knot down to your work so it is right by the bead the thread is coming out of.

7. Make sure the knot is snug.

8. Put your needle on the two even loose ends.

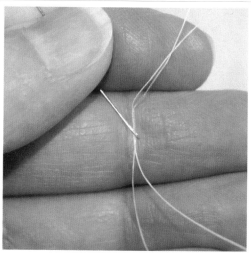

9. Work your needle forward through the beadwork, in the direction in which you were working.

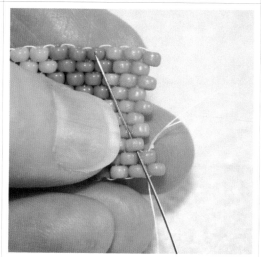

10. Continue working through each up and down bead until the last up bead before the end of the row.

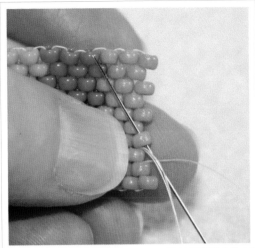

11. Trim the ends, making sure you do not cut the original threads below.

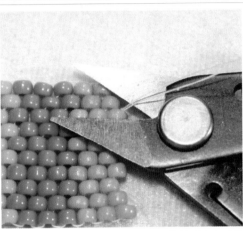

Peyote Stitch Bracelet

In this tutorial, I will describe the steps to make a very simple bracelet, using *peyote* stitch.

Table of Contents

Supplies

In addition to a needle and thread, you will need the following supplies for the bracelet:
- **8/0** seed beads - 5 grams of each of 4 colors (20 grams total)
  For the bracelet pictured in this tutorial, I used Miyuki 8-404, 8-416, 8-417L, and 8-4454.
- Toggle clasp

Peyote Patterns

When you start a peyote beading project, unless you are creating your own design, you will be working from a *pattern.* Most patterns contain the following elements:

- Image of the pattern, hopefully a photo of a beaded piece
- List of beads needed for the project (name and number of each bead)
- Bead graph, a detailed image that shows each bead color and placement
- Word chart, a line-by-line list of how many and in what order beads should be placed

For this tutorial, we will be using a very simple design, where each row is all one bead color, in groups of several rows of each color. Instructions for using a peyote pattern will be included in a later tutorial.

1 Prepare Your Work Area

Assemble your beads and tools. Make sure you have a good lighting source, if possible above and to the side.

2 Thread Your Needle

The amount of thread to use to start is a personal preference. Some people like to use a very long length so they don't have to add thread as often, but I find that my thread tends to tangle if I do this.

1. Pull a length of thread to match the length between your outstretched arms and cut from the spool.
2. Get a length of tape from the spool, about 1.5 inches long, and place it under the thread, about 12 inches from the end.

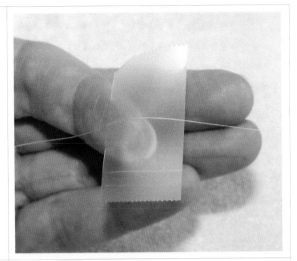

3. Double the tape over the thread so it sticks to itself.

4. Use your flat nose pliers to flatten the other end of the thread.

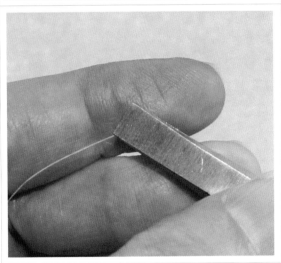

5. Work the thread onto your needle by holding the thread between the fingers of your left hand (or right if you are left-handed), and use your other hand to guide the needle onto the thread.

6. Make sure you have about 12 inches of thread doubled from the head of the needle so the thread doesn't slide off the needle while you are working. This amount will lessen as you progress through your beading and bead the doubled part of the thread.

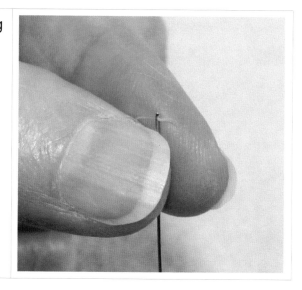

3 Start Your First Two Rows

The beads for the first two rows of peyote stitch are all put on the thread at one time.

1. Pile together 10 beads of your first bead color.

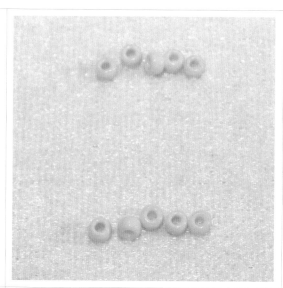

2. Pick up 5 beads onto your needle and bring them to the thread.

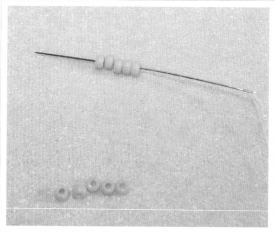

3. Pick up the other 5 beads onto your needle and bring all the beads down to the tape at the other end of your thread.

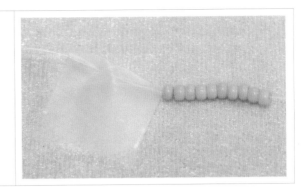

4 Bead Row Number 3

The first few rows are the most difficult in peyote so hang in there -- it gets much easier after that!

The first 10 beads you picked up represent 2 rows of peyote beading. It will become clear why that is in a bit. Next, gather together another 5 beads of the same color.

1. Hold your beadwork between the thumb and forefinger of your left hand (or right hand if you are left-handed).
2. Pick up one bead on your needle.
3. Work the needle UP through the second bead on the thread, trying to keep the first bead in position.
4. Pull your thread through.

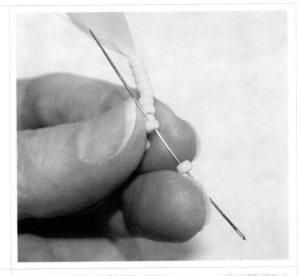

5. The beads should sit side by side, as shown in this photo. You may need to use your fingers to work them into place.

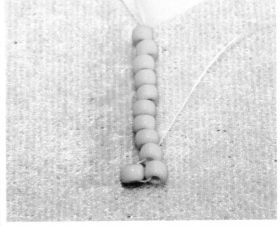

6. Pick up another bead on your needle and pull it down to your work.
7. Skip one bead (very important!) and work your needle up through the next bead.
8. Pull your thread through.

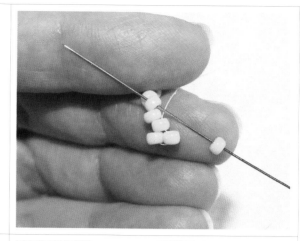

9. Your beadwork should look like this photo.
10. Continue picking up one bead, skipping one bead, and working your needle UP through the next bead in line until you reach the end of the row.

11. Your beadwork should now look like this.

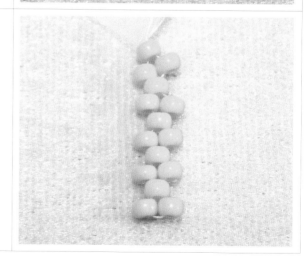

5 Bead Row Numbers 4 through 6

The beading should start to get easier now. Try not to twist your work. Press it flat as you go if that helps.

1. Turn your work over so the tape is now at the bottom of the work.
2. Holding your work between your second and third fingers, start at the tape end.
3. Pick up one bead.
4. Work your needle UP through the second bead in line, which is the first "up" bead of the third row.
5. Pull your thread through.

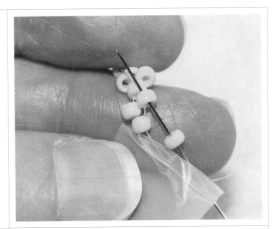

6. Pick up another bead and continue that process of working the needle through the next "up" bead and pulling the thread through until you reach the end of the row.

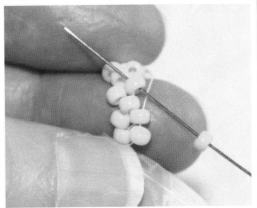

7. At the end of the row, your work should look like this.

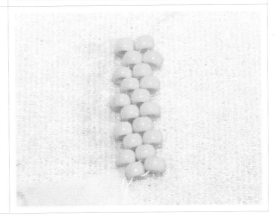

8. Bead 2 more rows by flipping your work before each new row and following step 6.

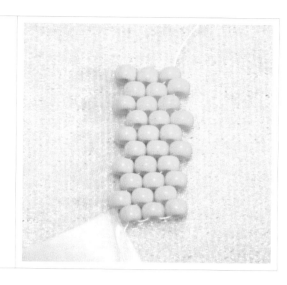

6 Add a New Color

For this bracelet we are going to bead 6 rows of each color. It's time to move on to our second color.

1. Pick up a bead from your second color and start the new row with it.

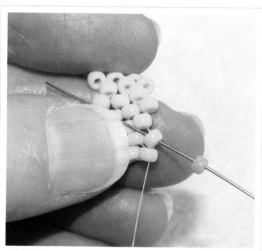

2. Continue adding beads in the new color.

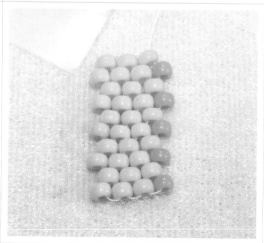

3. Continue until you have beaded 6 rows of the new color.

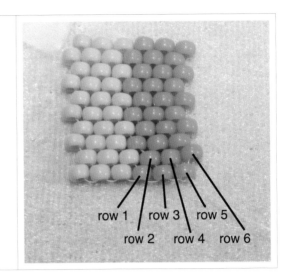

row 1　row 3　row 5

row 2　row 4　row 6

7 Continue Adding Six Rows of Each Color

1. Add 6 rows of color number 3.

2. Add 6 rows of color number 4.

3. Start back with color number 1.

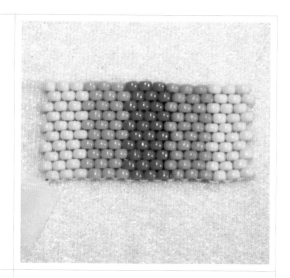

4. Continue adding 6 rows of each color in the same order (color 1, color 2, color 3, color 4). As you continue adding rows, move your needle down the thread so you are always only bringing a single thread through after you add a bead.

When your **thread** is about 10 inches long (or 5 inches doubled), it is time to add new thread. See the Introduction for instructions on how to add thread.

8 Add Loop End of Clasp

For this project, we are using a toggle clasp. First we will add the loop end of the clasp.

1. Work your way through beads to get to the center of the outer edge.

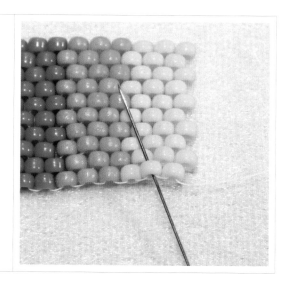

 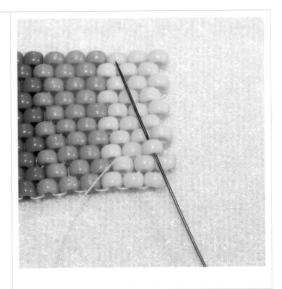

2. Pick up a bead and add it between two beads on the center end. This will provide a spot for the clasp to attach.

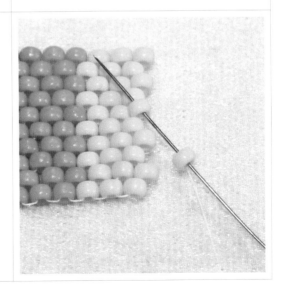

3. Work through the beads until you are coming back through the bead you just added.

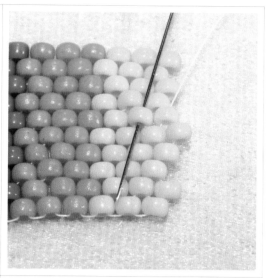

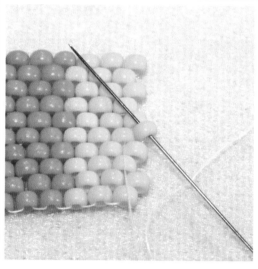

4. Pick up the loop end of your clasp.

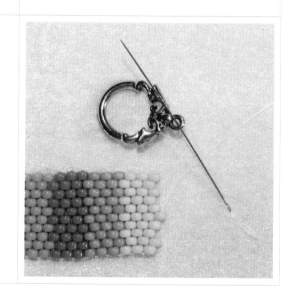

5. Run your needle back UP through the bead your thread is coming out of.

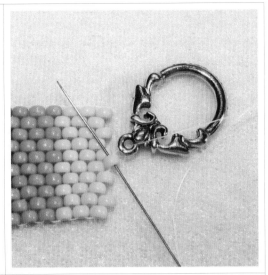

6. Run your needle UP through the bead above your current bead.

7. Work through the beads surrounding the anchor point. You want to secure the thread through them.

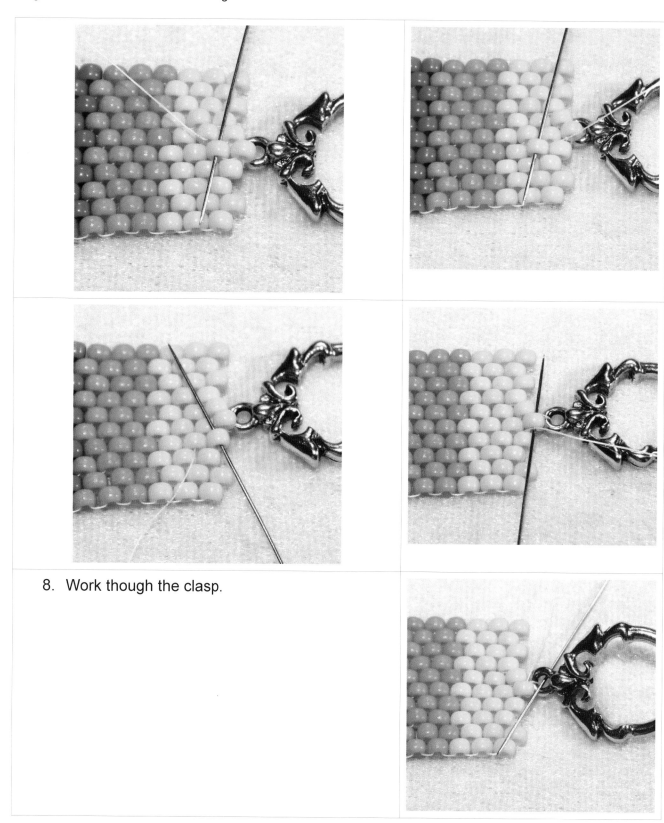

8. Work though the clasp.

9. Go back through the outer bead from the opposite direction so the clasp will be attached from both sides of the outer bead.
10. Go through the same path as in Steps 6 and 7 again to secure the clasp.

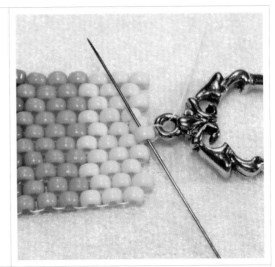

11. Work through at least 10 beads to firmly anchor your thread.

12. Continue in the opposite direction as needed.

13. Trim the end of your thread close to the work.

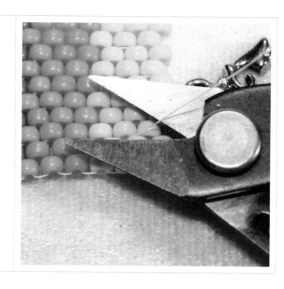

9 Add Toggle End of Clasp

Now we will add the toggle end of the clasp.

1. Remove the tape and put your needle on the tail thread on the other end of the bracelet.
2. Start working your way to the outer center, the same way as you did on the other end.

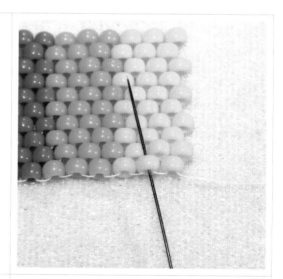

3. Stop when you get to this bead.

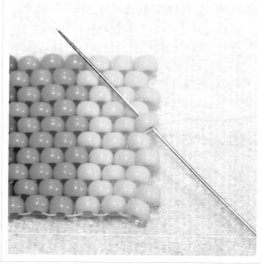

4. Pick up 6 beads of the same color you are coming out of and bring them down to your work. This will be the stem for the toggle. Without the stem, you cannot get the toggle through the loop while putting the bracelet on. I'll bet you can guess how I figured out that you need a stem!

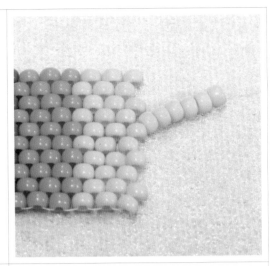

5. Go back through the bead you just came out of, from the opposite side.

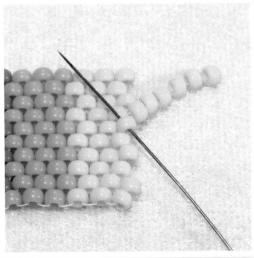

6. Turn your work and go up through 3 of the beads you added for the stem.

7. Go through the toggle eye.

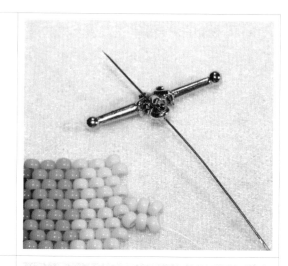

8. Go down through the other 3 beads you added for the stem.

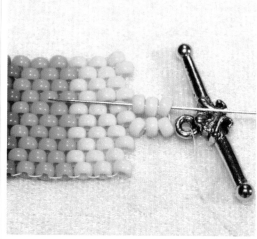

9. Go through the bead below the stem beads.

10. Go back through the stem beads and the toggle eye, making sure you go through the eye in the location that pins it to both sides of the stem beads.

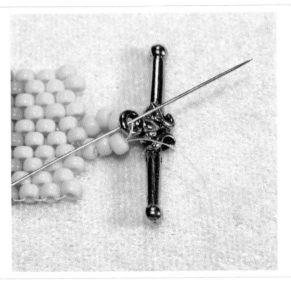

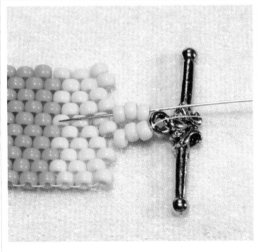

11. Go back through the bead below the stem.

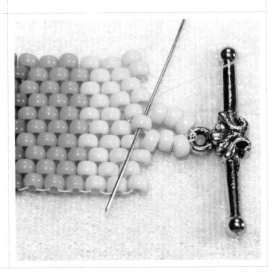

12. Go back through at least 10 beads on the bracelet to make sure your thread is firmly anchored.

13. Trim the thread end.

Congratulations! Your bracelet is finished!

Peyote Pen Wrap

In this tutorial, I will describe the steps to make a beaded pen wrap, including learning to read a peyote stitch pattern and word chart.

Debbie van Tonder graciously allowed me to use her "Jigsaw-Puzzle" design for this tutorial. Please do not post or give the pattern away.

Contents

Supplies

- **Beads**: Delica 11/0 seed beads (chart later in this section)
- **Thread**: FireLine 6lb thread (crystal)
- **Pen**: Pilot G2.
  You can use any color pen you want. I will use a black pen for this tutorial.

In this project, we will be using a pattern that includes a list of the beads you will need and the number of each color. Here is the Bead Legend for the pattern we are using:

Chart #:A
DB-658
Opaque Turquoise Green
Count:168

Chart #:B
DB-730
Opaque Light Sapphire
Count:127

Chart #:C
DB-733
Chartreuse Opaque
Count:181

Chart #:D
DB-751
Yellow Opaque Matte
Count:127

Chart #:E
DB-752
Matte Opaque Orange
Count:181

Chart #:F
DB-757
Matte Opaque Light Siam
Count:140

- **Chart # and a letter**: The pattern author can choose to use numbers or letters or both. All letters is easiest to follow. When we lay out our beads, we will put a letter indicator next to each color so we know which is which.
- **DB- and a number**: This is the unique number given to the color by the bead manufacturer (Miyuki).
- **Color name**: The manufacturer does not provide color names so they vary from vendor to vendor. DB-10 is always black, because that's easy, but DB-723 can be Opaque Dark Cranberry or Opaque Red or whatever the vendor chooses to call it. You can see where the bead number (DB-723) is really important to know since the color name can be pretty much anything.
- **Count**: This is the number of beads of each color needed to complete the design in the pattern. Different Delica beads have slightly different weights because of the different materials and coatings. I have found 190 beads per gram to be a good number for estimating. Delica packages typically come in 7.5 grams or 50 grams but some vendors allow you to pick smaller or larger numbers of grams.

Based on approximately 190 Delica beads per gram, for this project you will need:

Delica Item Number	Number of Beads	Number of Grams
DB-658	168	1
DB-730	127	1
DB-733	181	1
DB-751	127	1
DB-752	181	1
DB-757	140	1

Peyote Patterns

When working a peyote beading project, unless you are creating your own design, you will be working from a *pattern*. Most patterns contain the following elements:

- Image of the pattern, often a photo of a beaded piece
- List of beads needed for the project (name and count for each bead color)
- *Bead* chart, a detailed image that shows each bead color and placement
- *Word* chart, a line by line list of how many and in what order beads should be placed

There are two methods for following a peyote beading pattern. The method you choose depends on personal preference. Try each method and figure out which one works better for you.

Note: All peyote beadwork is started with the first two rows of beads placed on the thread together.

How to Read a Peyote *Bead* Chart

Some patterns only come with a bead chart and not a word chart, so even if you prefer using a word chart, sometimes you need to know how to work from a bead chart. Following are the steps to work from a **bead chart**.

1. Place your ruler under the second row of the bead chart, which also places the ruler in the middle of the third row, which you can ignore for now.

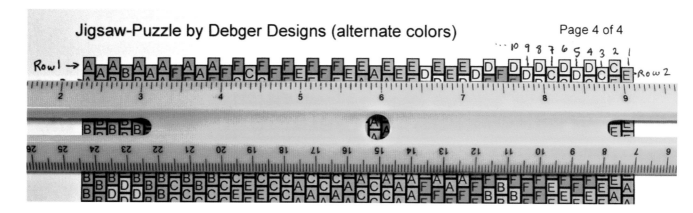

2. Pick your beads from your piles and place them in order on your mat. In this case, you will start on the **right**, looking left, and pick up (1)E, (2)C, (3)D, (1)C, (3)D, and so on, where 3(D) means 3 beads of color D. You will be picking up one bead from the first row, then one bead from the second row, and so on. You will only be doing this for the first two rows of your peyote beadwork.
3. Once you have picked up all the beads for the first two rows, add them to your thread, in the *exact* order that you picked them up.
4. After you place the beads for Rows 1 and 2 on your thread, move the ruler down to just below row 3.
5. The beads for Row 3 are every other bead in the diagram. In this case, they are: (1)A, (2)B, (1)A, (2)F, (2)C, and so on. (2)C means 2 beads of color C.
6. Place all the beads for Row 3 on your mat, in order, and bead them as the third row of your peyote beadwork.
7. After you complete Row 3, move the ruler down to just below Row 4 and repeat the steps you did in Row 3, using the beads called for in the bead chart for Row 4.
8. Continue on for all remaining rows, adding thread as needed.

Important Note: Note the "down" bead on the upper *right* corner of the bead chart. Note the "up" bead on the upper *left* corner of the bead chart. If the down bead is on the left instead of the right, then start counting the beads for the first two rows on the left instead of on the right. If there are up beads or down beads on both end, then this is an odd count peyote pattern and it doesn't matter which end you start counting for your first two rows. Odd count peyote will be covered in a later tutorial. It requires an additional beading technique over even count peyote.

How to Read a Peyote *Word* Chart

I personally find a word chart much easier to work from than a bead chart, but there are many people who feel exactly the opposite. Here are the steps to work from a word chart.

1. Place your ruler under the line marked "Row 1&2". In some rare instances, the author does not merge Rows 1 and 2, and you will need to use the method described above to read the bead chart to lay out the beads for Rows 1 and 2.

Jigsaw-Puzzle by Debger Designs (alternate colors)   Page 2 of 4

Row 1&2 (L) (1)E, (2)C, (3)D, (1)C, (3)D, (1)F, (2)D, (3)E, (1)D, (3)E, (1)A, (2)E, (3)F, (1)E, (3)F, (1)C, (2)F, (3)A, (1)F, (3)A, (1)B, (3)A

Row 5 (R) (1)   )E, (

Row 8 (L) (4)E, (5)F, (5)A, (5)C, (3)B
Row 9 (R) (4)B, (5)C, (5)A, (5)F, (3)E

2. Lay out the beads as described in the word chart: (1)E, (2)C, (3)D, (1)C, (3)D, and so on, where 3(D) means 3 beads of color D.
3. String all the beads for Rows 1 and 2 in the exact order in which you laid them out.
4. Move your ruler down to Row 3 on your word chart.
5. Row 3 starts with (1)A, (2)B, (1)A, (2)F, (2)C, and so on, where (2)C means 2 beads of color C. Place all the beads for Row 3 on your mat, in order, and bead them as the third row of your peyote beadwork.
6. After you complete Row 3, move the ruler down to just below Row 4 and repeat the steps you did in Row 3, using the beads called for in the word chart for Row 4.
7. Continue on for all remaining rows, adding thread as needed.

1 Prepare Your Work Area

Assemble the tools you need for this project.

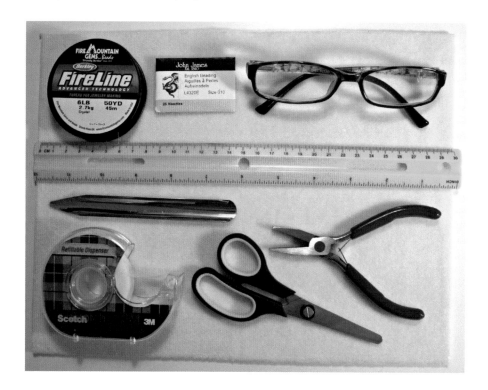

Line up the beads for this project and put a tag next to each color with the letter used in the Bead Legend.

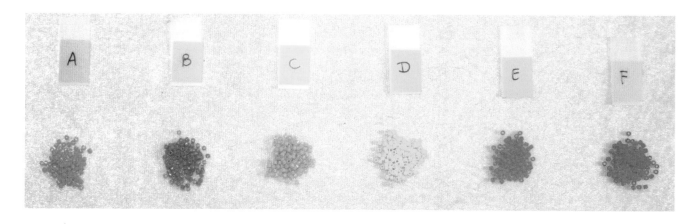

2 Start Your First Two Rows

The beads for the first two rows of peyote stitch are all put on the thread at one time.

1. Thread your needle. I use tape in place of a stop bead about 8 inches from the end of the thread.
2. Lay out the beads for your first two rows, using either the bead graph or bead chart method, whichever you prefer.

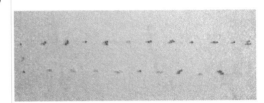

Note: When there are too many beads to lay in just one row, start the beginning beads in the row nearest to you and then start another row behind it on your mat. Based on experience, I know if you put the beginning row in the back, you will scatter the beads in the front row as you pick them up.

3. Pick up the first 5 beads at a time, ***in order***.

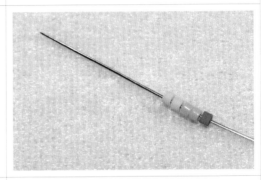

4. Bring those beads down to the tape on the end of the thread.

5. Continue picking up about 5 beads at a time, *in order,* and bringing them to bottom of the thread until you have all the beads for Rows 1 and 2 on your thread.

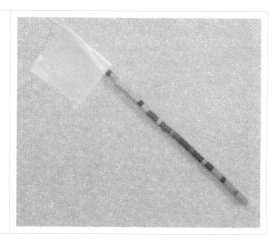

3 Bead Row Number 3

The first few rows are the most difficult in peyote so hang in there -- it gets much easier after that!

1. Lay out the beads for Row 3, following the bead or word chart.	
2. Hold your beadwork between the thumb and forefinger of your left hand (or right hand if you are left-handed). 3. To start Row 3, pick up the first bead from your mat and put it on your needle. 4. Work the needle up through the second bead on the thread, trying to keep the first bead in position. 5. Pull your thread through.	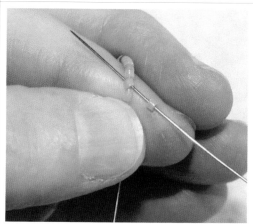
6. The beads should sit side by side, as shown in this photo. You may need to use your fingers to work them into place.	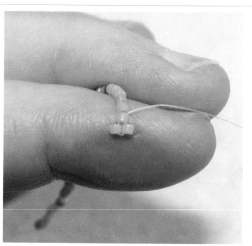

7. Pick up another bead on your needle and pull it down to your work.
8. Skip one bead (very important!) and work your needle up through the next bead.
9. Pull your thread through.

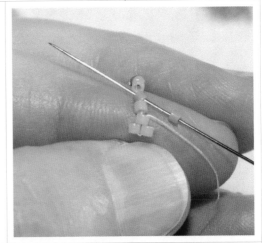

10. Your beadwork should look like this photo.
11. Continue picking up one bead, skipping one bead, and working your needle through the next bead in line until you reach the end of the row.

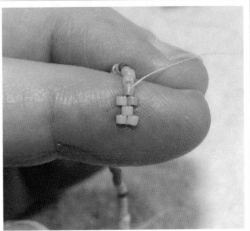

12. Your beadwork should now look like this.

Important: It is okay if the beadwork is curling a bit. However, make sure that you keep it flat and with the Row 3 beads on the right so it will be in the right order when you add the Row 4 beads. It helps to lay your work on the table and flatten it if you can, making sure the beads stay in order.

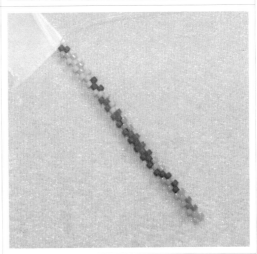

4 Bead Additional Rows

The beading should start to get easier now. Try not to twist your work. Press it flat as you go if that helps.

1. Lay out the beads for the next row.
2. Turn your work over so the tape is now at the bottom of the work.

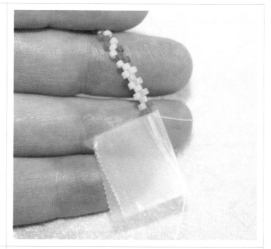

3. Holding your work between your second and third fingers, start at the tape end.
4. Pick up one bead.
5. Work your needle through the second bead in line, which is the first "up" bead of the third row.
6. Pull your thread through.
7. Pick up another bead and continue that process of working the needle through the next "up" bead and pulling the thread through until you reach the end of the row.

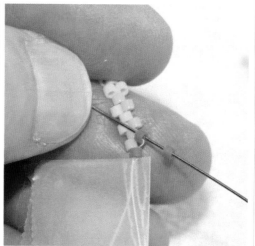

8. At the end of the row, your work should look like this.

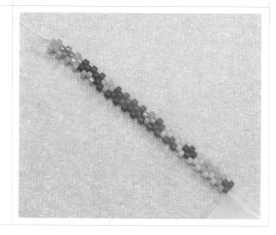

9. Repeat steps 1 through 7 for additional rows. As you continue beading, it becomes easier to see how the rows are laid out and numbered.

10. Continue until you have beaded all the rows in the pattern, adding thread as needed.

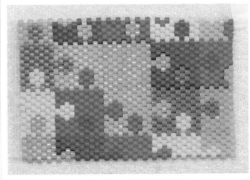

5 Weave in Your Tail Thread

Since we are not adding a clasp to this piece, we can weave in the tail thread.

1. Remove your needle from your work thread.
2. Remove the tape from your tail thread.
3. Put your needle on your tail thread.
4. Start weaving your tail thread in by running your needle UP through the edge bead next to the bead your thread is coming out of.

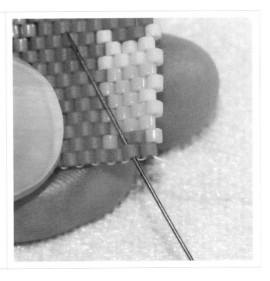

5. Continue weaving your tail thread in by running your needle UP through the next bead up and to the right as you move towards the end of your beadwork.

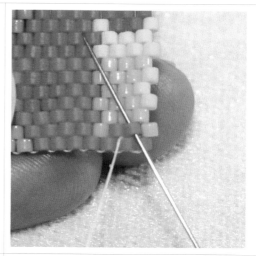

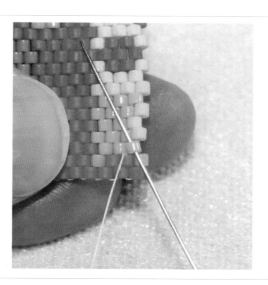

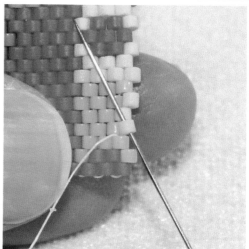

6. Continue moving your needle through beads along the end of your beadwork, inner and outside in sequence until you have about 2-inches of thread woven through the end beads.

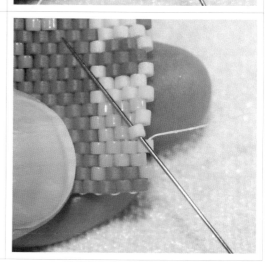

7. Carefully trim off the excess trail thread, being sure not to cut the weaving threads.

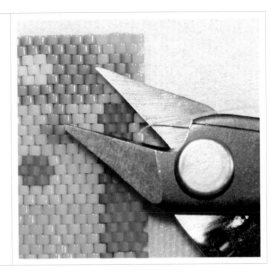

6 Zip Up Beadwork

We will connect the edges of your beadwork together using a method sometimes called zipping up.

1. Put your needle back on your work thread.
2. Compare your beaded panel to the pattern picture to make sure they are oriented the same way. Check the upper corners to make sure they match the pattern picture.

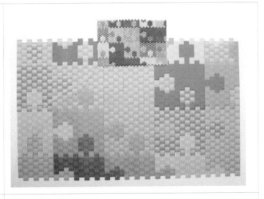

3. Curl the panel over your finger so it maintains that image orientation for the outside of the curl.

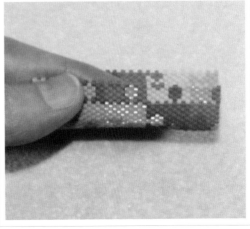

4. Line up the edges of the panel and run your needle DOWN through the bead opposite the end bead where the thread is coming out. Pull thread through to snug.

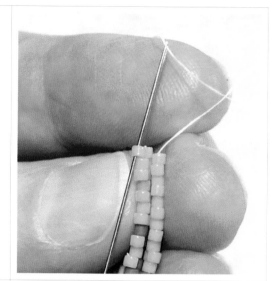

5. Run your needle back UP through the opposite bead, that is the bead where you started. We are going back around to reinforce the end stitches. Pull thread through to snug.

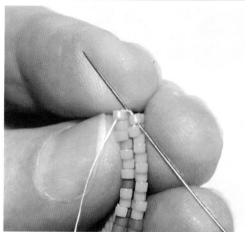

6. Run your needle DOWN through the top left bead one more time to complete the reinforcement. Pull thread through to snug.

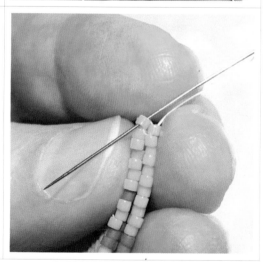

7. Run your needle DOWN through the opposite bead, down one column from the beading you are coming out of. When you pull the thread through you can see the start of the zipping operation.

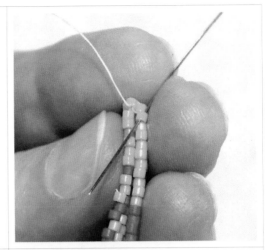

8. Run your needle DOWN through the opposite bead, on the left, down one column from the beading you are coming out of. Pull thread through to snug.

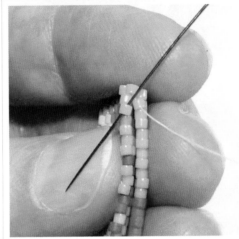

9. Continue moving through the opposite side bead, down one column.

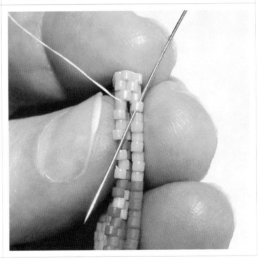

10. When you get to the end of the row, your zipped piece will look like this.

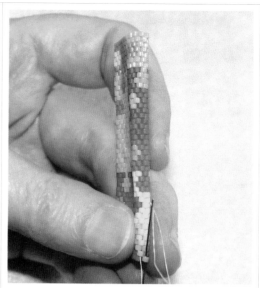

11. As you did with the bead at the top of this row, go back UP through to secure the bottom two beads.

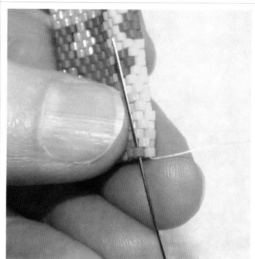

12. Go DOWN through the next bead to start weaving in your tail.
13. Continue going up and down through the edge beads for at least 10 stitches to secure your tail.

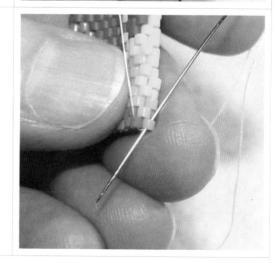

14. If you are not planning on adding the (optional) edging beads, trim the end of the tail without cutting any of the weaving threads and then go to Section 8 of this tutorial.

7 Optional: Add Edging Beads

Although the pen wrap is fine as it is, if there is enough room, you can add edging beads to cover the stitching and give the pen wrap an extra finished look.

1. Make sure your thread is coming out of the edge of your beadwork.
2. Pick up an edging bead and go DOWN through the next bead to the right.

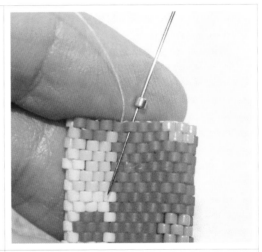

3. Run the needle UP to the bead to the right.

4. Pick up an edging bead and go DOWN through the next bead to the right.

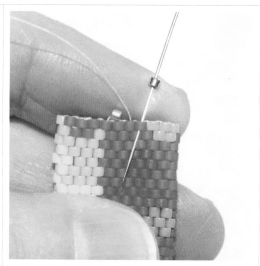

5. Run the needle UP through the bead to the right.

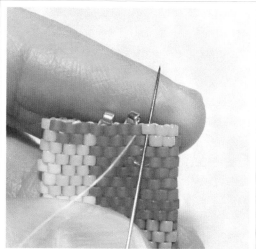

6. Continue adding beads as in steps 4 and 5 until you run out of space to add more.
7. Your last up will be to the right of the first edging bead you added.

8. Run your needle through the two beads above and to the left of the location where your thread is coming out.

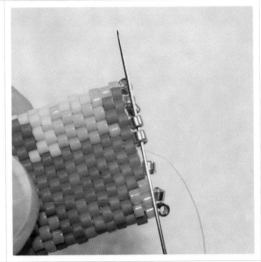

9. Pick up 2 edging beads and run your needle UP through the next edging bead.

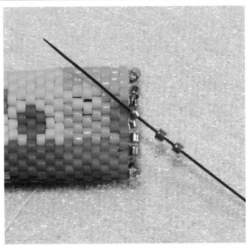

10. Pick up 1 edging bead and run your needle UP through the next edging bead.

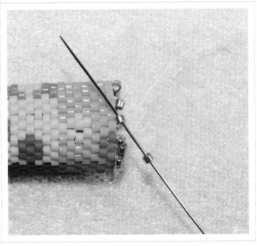

11. Repeat steps 9 and 10, between picking up 2 and 1 edging beads and running your needle UP through the next edging bead until you come to the location where you started.
12. Run your needle UP through 2 beads (without picking up a new bead).

13. Continue running your needle left through several beads at a time (2 to 4 beads, depending on what feels comfortable) until you have gone through all the beads at least twice. This is going to anchor your thread and give the edging beads a finished look.
14. When you have finished going through the edging beads at least twice, trim the thread close to your work, taking care not to cut any beadwork threads.
15. Turn the bead wrap and repeat the steps for adding the edging beads and anchoring your thread to the other end.

8 Wrap Beadwork Around Pen

1. Unscrew the top from the Pilot G2 pen.

2. Very gently, start to work the pen barrel into the beadwork tube. Twisting a bit, again gently, helps.	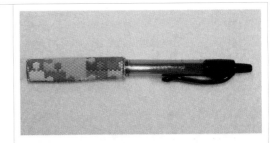
3. Continue gently twisting and pushing until the pen barrel is completely covered by the beadwork tube.	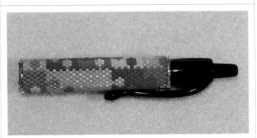
4. Insert the ink cartridge side of the pen into the pen barrel.	
5. Screw the bottom half of the pen into the top half until snug.	

Congratulations! Your pen wrap is finished!

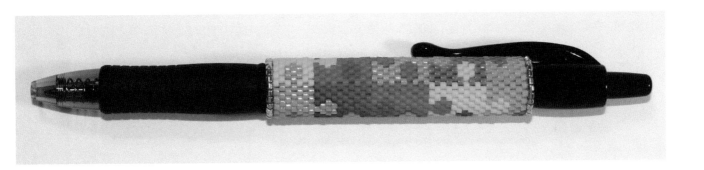

Project Pattern

Jigsaw-Puzzle by Debger Designs (alternate colors)   Page 1

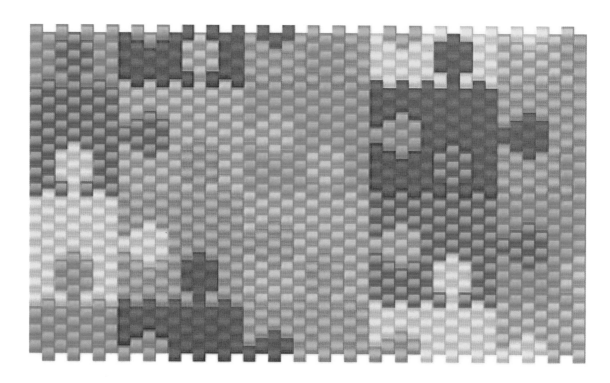

▯ Chart #:A DB-658 Opaque Turquoise Green Count:168	▯ Chart #:B DB-730 Opaque Light Sapphire Count:127	▯ Chart #:C DB-733 Chartreuse Opaque Count:181
▯ Chart #:D DB-751 Yellow Opaque Matte Count:127	▯ Chart #:E DB-752 Matte Opaque Orange Count:181	▯ Chart #:F DB-757 Matte Opaque Light Siam Count:140

Jigsaw-Puzzle by Debger Designs (alternate colors)   Page 2

Row 1&2 (L) (1)E, (2)C, (3)D, (1)C, (3)D, (1)F, (2)D, (3)E, (1)D, (3)E, (1)A, (2)E, (3)F, (1)E, (3)F, (1)C, (2)F, (3)A, (1)F, (3)A, (1)B, (3)A

Row 3 (R) (1)A, (2)B, (1)A, (2)F, (2)C, (1)F, (2)E, (2)A, (1)E, (2)D, (2)F, (1)D, (2)C, (1)E

Row 4 (L) (1)E, (3)C, (1)D, (1)F, (3)D, (1)E, (1)A, (3)E, (1)F, (1)C, (3)F, (1)A, (1)B, (1)A

Row 5 (R) (1)A, (2)B, (1)A, (2)F, (2)C, (1)F, (2)E, (2)A, (1)E, (2)D, (2)F, (1)D, (2)C, (1)E

Row 6 (L) (1)E, (3)C, (1)D, (1)F, (3)D, (1)E, (1)A, (3)E, (1)F, (1)C, (3)F, (1)A, (1)B, (1)A

Row 7 (R) (4)A, (5)F, (5)E, (5)D, (3)C

Row 8 (L) (4)E, (5)F, (5)A, (5)C, (3)B

Row 9 (R) (4)B, (5)C, (5)A, (5)F, (3)E

Row 10 (L) (4)E, (5)F, (5)A, (5)C, (3)B

Row 11 (R) (4)B, (5)C, (5)A, (5)F, (3)E

Row 12 (L) (2)E, (1)F, (1)E, (3)F, (1)A, (1)F, (3)A, (1)C, (1)A, (3)C, (1)B, (1)C, (3)B

Row 13 (R) (6)B, (5)C, (5)A, (5)F, (1)E

Row 14 (L) (2)E, (5)F, (5)A, (5)C, (5)B

Row 15 (R) (6)B, (5)C, (5)A, (5)F, (1)E

Row 16 (L) (1)A, (1)E, (1)F, (1)E, (1)F, (1)B, (1)F, (1)A, (1)F, (1)A, (1)C, (1)A, (1)C, (1)A, (1)C, (1)E, (1)C, (1)B, (1)C, (1)B, (1)D, (1)B

Row 17 (R) (1)B, (2)D, (1)B, (2)C, (2)E, (1)C, (2)A, (2)C, (1)A, (2)F, (2)B, (1)F, (2)E, (1)A

Row 18 (L) (1)A, (3)E, (1)F, (1)B, (3)F, (1)A, (1)C, (3)A, (1)C, (1)E, (3)C, (1)B, (1)D, (1)B

Row 19 (R) (1)B, (2)D, (1)B, (2)C, (2)E, (1)C, (2)A, (2)C, (1)A, (2)F, (2)B, (1)F, (2)E, (1)A

Row 20 (L) (1)A, (3)E, (1)F, (1)B, (3)F, (1)A, (1)C, (3)A, (1)C, (1)E, (3)C, (1)B, (1)D, (1)B

Row 21 (R) (4)B, (5)C, (5)A, (5)F, (3)E

Row 22 (L) (4)A, (5)B, (5)C, (5)E, (3)D

Row 23 (R) (4)D, (5)E, (5)C, (5)B, (3)A

Row 24 (L) (4)A, (5)B, (5)C, (5)E, (3)D

Row 25 (R) (4)D, (5)E, (5)C, (5)B, (3)A

Row 26 (L) (2)A, (1)B, (1)A, (3)B, (1)C, (1)B, (3)C, (1)E, (1)C, (3)E, (1)D, (1)E, (3)D

Row 27 (R) (6)D, (5)E, (5)C, (5)B, (1)A

Row 28 (L) (2)A, (5)B, (5)C, (5)E, (5)D

Row 29 (R) (6)D, (5)E, (5)C, (5)B, (1)A

Row 30 (L) (1)C, (1)A, (1)B, (1)A, (1)B, (1)D, (1)B, (1)C, (1)B, (1)C, (1)E, (1)C, (1)E, (1)C, (1)E, (1)F, (1)E, (1)D, (1)E, (1)D, (1)A, (1)D

Row 31 (R) (1)D, (2)A, (1)D, (2)E, (2)F, (1)E, (2)C, (2)E, (1)C, (2)B, (2)D, (1)B, (2)A, (1)C

Row 32 (L) (1)C, (3)A, (1)B, (1)D, (3)B, (1)C, (1)E, (3)C, (1)E, (1)F, (3)E, (1)D, (1)A, (1)D

Row 33 (R) (1)D, (2)A, (1)D, (2)E, (2)F, (1)E, (2)C, (2)E, (1)C, (2)B, (2)D, (1)B, (2)A, (1)C

Jigsaw-Puzzle by Debger Designs (alternate colors)   Page 3

Row 34 (L) (1)C, (3)A, (1)B, (1)D, (3)B, (1)C, (1)E, (3)C, (1)E, (1)F, (3)E, (1)D, (1)A, (1)D

Row 35 (R) (4)D, (5)E, (5)C, (5)B, (3)A

Row 36 (L) (4)C, (5)D, (5)E, (5)F, (3)A

Row 37 (R) (4)A, (5)F, (5)E, (5)D, (3)C

Row 38 (L) (4)C, (5)D, (5)E, (5)F, (3)A

Row 39 (R) (4)A, (5)F, (5)E, (5)D, (3)C

Row 40 (L) (2)C, (1)D, (1)C, (3)D, (1)E, (1)D, (3)E, (1)F, (1)E, (3)F, (1)A, (1)F, (3)A

Row 41 (R) (6)A, (5)F, (5)E, (5)D, (1)C

Row 42 (L) (2)C, (5)D, (5)E, (5)F, (5)A

Jigsaw-Puzzle by Debger Designs (alternate colors)

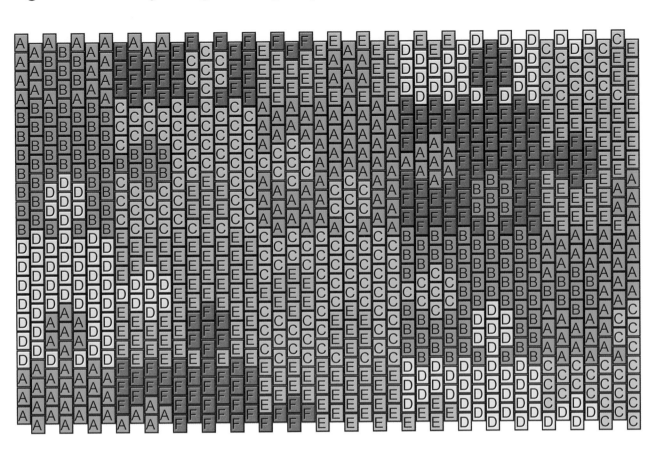

Odd Count Peyote Bracelet

Peyote stitch is known for the offset rows it creates. Most people learn *even* count peyote first. As the name implies, it includes an even number of beads across each row. If you want to center a design around a central column, you need to use *odd* count peyote, which means there is one additional bead in each row. You use a special technique to add that extra bead. In this tutorial, we will describe the steps to make a very simple odd count peyote bracelet with a picot edge and a slide clasp.

Table of Contents

Supplies and Pattern

This bracelet is 15 columns wide by 104 rows long. It uses 6 different colors of size 8/0 seed beads:

- **8/0** seed beads
  - Color A - 3 grams (Miyuki 8-404)
  - Color B - 4 grams (Miyuki 8-406)
  - Color C - 2 grams (Miyuki 8-411)
  - Color D - 2 grams (Miyuki 8-413)
  - Color E - 3 grams (Miyuki 8-416)
  - Color F - 3 grams (Miyuki 8-1477)
- **11/0** seed beads for the picot edging (2 grams of a color that goes well with the body of the bracelet; we used galvanized gold for the tutorial)
- 3-strand slide **clasp**

Follow the pattern called *Chevrons* (at the end of this lesson) for this tutorial. The pattern is for a 6.5 inch bracelet. You can make it longer by repeating the pattern and of course you will need more beads.

1 Prepare Your Work Area

Assemble the tools you need for this project.

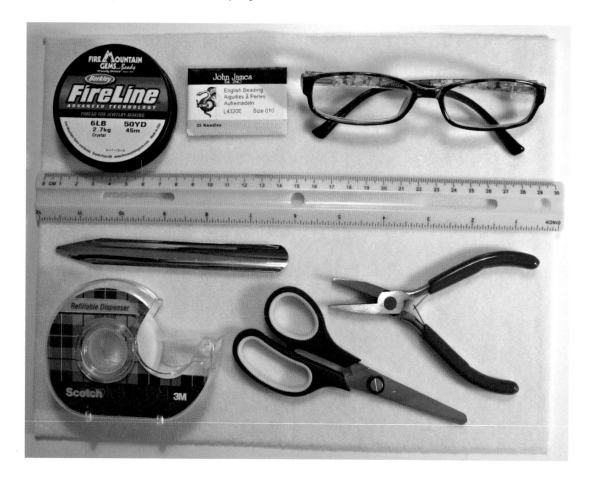

Using the *Chevrons* pattern as a guide, line up the beads for this project, in the order in which they are shown in the Bead Legend, and put a tag next to each color with the appropriate letter.

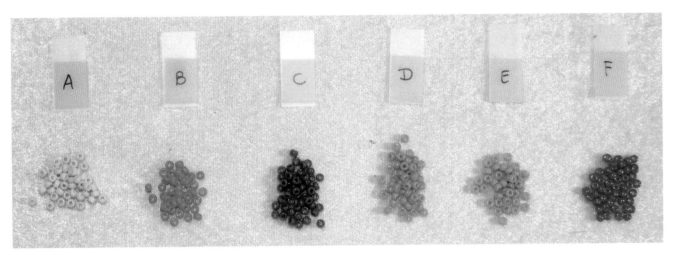

2 Start Your First Two Rows

The beads for the first two rows of peyote stitch are all put on the thread at one time.

1. Thread your needle. I use tape in place of a stop bead about 10 inches from the end of the thread.
2. Lay out the beads for your first two rows, using either the bead graph or bead chart method, whichever you prefer.

Note: When there are too many beads to lay in just one row, start the beginning beads in the row nearest to you and then start another row behind it on your mat. Based on experience, I know if I put the beginning row in the back, I tend to scatter the beads in the front row as I pick the beginning beads up.

3. Pick up the beads for the first row. For this pattern, the first row is all the same color so order does not matter. Bring the beads to the tape until you have all the beads for Rows 1 and 2 on your thread.

3 Bead Row Number 3

The first few rows are the most difficult in peyote so hang in there — it gets much easier after that!

1. Lay out the beads for Row 3, following the bead or word chart.

2. Hold your beadwork between the thumb and forefinger of your left hand (or right hand if you are left-handed), with your third finger holding the back end of the work steady.
3. Pick up one bead on your needle.
4. Work the needle UP through the second bead on the thread, trying to keep the first bead in position.
5. Pull your thread through.

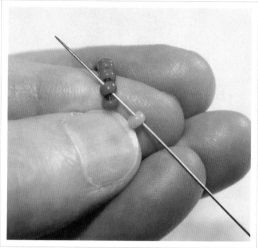

6. The beads should sit side by side, as shown in this photo. You may need to use your fingers to work them into place.

7. Pick up another bead on your needle and pull it down to your work.
8. Skip one bead (very important!) and work your needle UP through the next bead.
9. Pull your thread through.

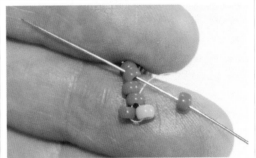

10. Continue picking up one bead, skipping one bead, and working your needle through the next bead in line until you have added the second to last bead.
11. Your beadwork should now look like this.

Notes:
- It's okay if the beadwork is curving a bit. It will straighten out when you add the next row.
- There is no "up" bead to connect the last bead you need to add.

4 Add Odd Count Bead

Here are the things to think about when adding the odd count bead:
1. First you pick up the odd bead and start anchoring it by going down through the last bead of the first row, the last bead of the second row, and the last bead of the current row.
2. Then you go up through the bead to the left of your current position, up through the center bead, and back up through the last bead of the first row.
3. Finally you go down through the bead you just added.

This technique, sometimes called "figure 8" because of the shape of the thread path, allows you to move through the beads in a way that shows no thread and gets you to the correct position to start the next row.

This may sound like a lot for adding one bead, but using this method assures that the bead sits in its proper place and it is well anchored to the beadwork. Picture the figure 8 in your head as you go. You will get used to adding the odd bead, which only happens every other row.
Let's do it!

1. Notice that there is no bead to anchor your last "odd" bead to.	
2. Pick up the last bead for the current row and run your needle DOWN through: 3. - The last bead of the first row. 4. - The last bead of the second row. 5. - The last bead you added for the current row. You are going DOWN through 3 beads at once.	

6. Use your left forefinger to nudge the new bead in place. This is what your beadwork should look like now, including where the thread is coming out.

7. Next run your needle UP through the bead to the left of the current bead.

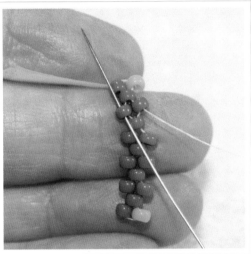

8. Run your needle UP through:
   - The bead above and to the right of the current bead.
   - The bead to the left of the bead you just added. You are going UP through 2 beads.

9. Run your needle DOWN through the odd count bead you added at the end of this row.
10. Your thread is now in the correct location to start adding beads for the next row.

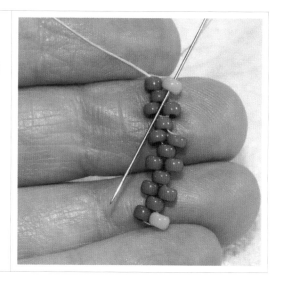

5 Bead Row Number 4

The even rows are just like "normal" peyote rows. You do not need to add the odd bead. Try not to twist your work. Press it flat as you go if that helps.

1. Lay out the beads for Row 4.
2. Turn your work over so the tape is now at the bottom of the work.
3. Holding your work between your second and third fingers, start at the tape end.
4. Pick up one bead.
5. Work your needle through the second bead in line, which is the first "up" bead of the third row.
6. Pull your thread through.

7. Pick up another bead and continue that process of working the needle through the next "up" bead and pulling the thread through until you reach the end of the row.

8. At the end of the row, your work should look like this.

6 Add Row Number 5 and Beyond

Repeat Sections 3 through 5 until you have added all the rows for the bracelet. Add thread as needed.

7 Add Picot Edging

We are going to add a picot edging to give our bracelet a finished look on the edges. With 3-bead picot edging, it works well to use a bead size slightly smaller than the body of the bracelet. In this case we are using 8/0 beads for the body, so we are going to use 11/0 beads for the picot edging.

1. Pick up 3 11/0 seed beads.

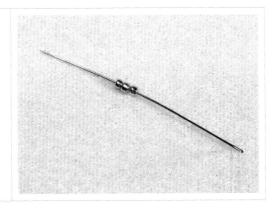

2. Run the needle **down** through the bead next to the bead where the thread is coming out.

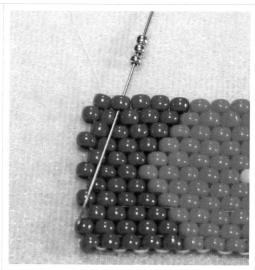

3. Run the needle **up** through the bead next to the bead where the thread is coming out.

4. Pick up 3 11/0 beads and run the needle DOWN through the bead next to the bead where the thread is coming out.

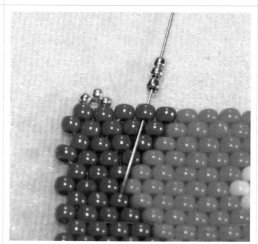

5. Run the needle UP through the bead next to the bead where the thread is coming out.

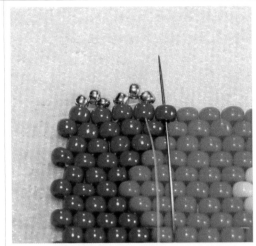

6. Repeat FireLines 4 and 5 until you reach the end of the bracelet side.
7. Notice that because of the number of rows in our bracelet, you have one bead that isn't part of a picot. Pick up 1 bead and go back down through the last bead of the last picot you added.

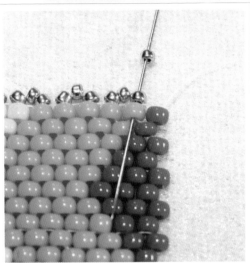

8. Run your needle down through the next bead near the top edge of your bracelet.

9. Run your needle down through the next bead and then repeat until you reach the end of the row.

10. Repeat Steps 4, 5, and 7 to add the picot edging to the other side.

11. Your bracelet should now look like this.

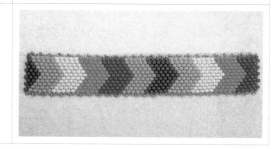

8 Add Clasp Side 1

We are going to use a 3-strand slide clasp, which looks like this. The narrow end of the clasp slides into the wider end of the clasp when the bracelet is worn.

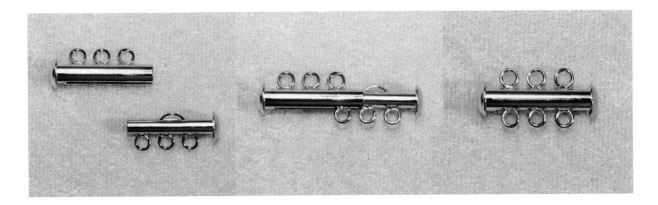

1. You want to center your clasp as well as possible on each end of the bracelet. Close up the clasp to check for centering and start attaching the clasp. The black lines in this photo show the points we will use to attach the clasp on this end.

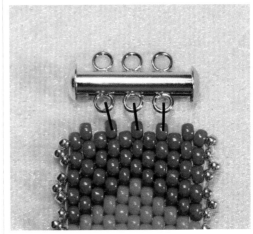

2. Run your needle DOWN through the bead below the bead where the thread is coming out.

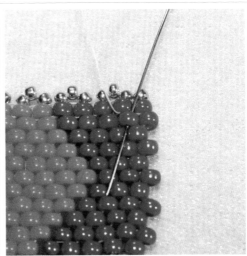

3. Run your needle DOWN through the bead below the bead where the thread is coming out.

4. Run your needle DOWN through the bead below the bead where the thread is coming out.

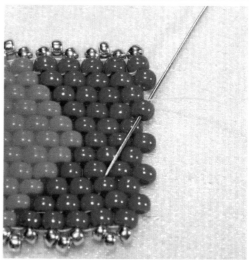

5. Pick up your closed clasp.
6. Run your needle through the clasp, from back to front.

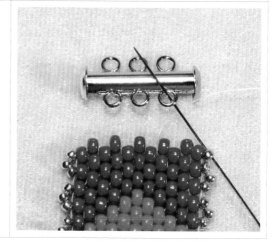

7. Run your needle back UP through the bead your thread is coming out of.

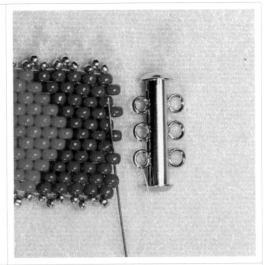

8. Run your needle UP through the bead above the current bead.

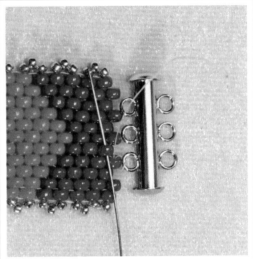

9. Run your needle UP through the next bead.

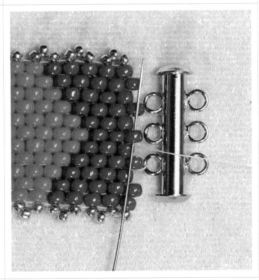

10. Repeat Steps 6 through 9 until all the loops are attached to your beadwork.

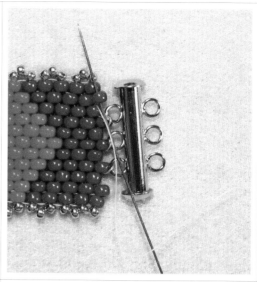

11. Run your needle DOWN through the bead to the left of the current bead. We are preparing to go back through all the loops to anchor them firmly.

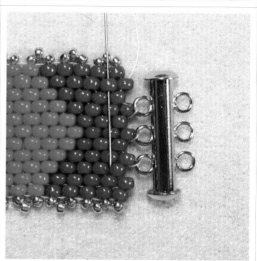

12. Run your needle DOWN through the bead below and to the right of the current bead.

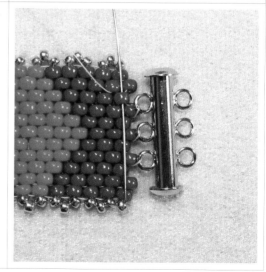

13. Run your needle DOWN through the bead below and to the right from the bead where your thread is coming out. This is the first bead attached to the clasp.

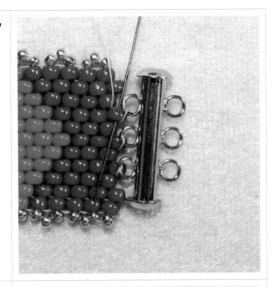

14. Run your needle UP through the loop.

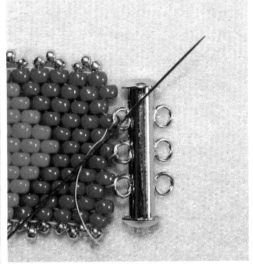

15. Run your needle DOWN through the bead your thread is coming out of.
16. As you did before, continue through the connecting beads to the next loop and so on until you have gone back through all 3 loops.

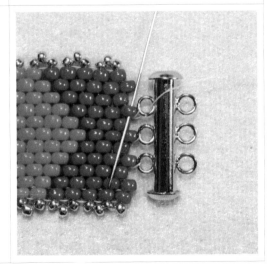

17. Weave your thread end up through beads to near the other edge of the bracelet, change direction, and back down a few beads to make sure the thread is anchored securely.
18. Trim the thread, being careful not to cut any threads in the beadwork.

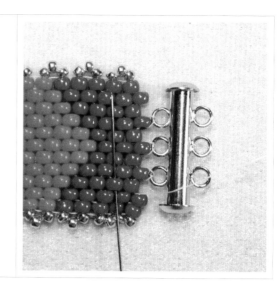

9 Add Clasp Side 2

1. If you have not already done so, remove the tape from your tail thread and put your needle on it.
2. For the second side of the clasp, it looks like the loops line up best with the spaces between the beads, rather than between the beads sticking out.

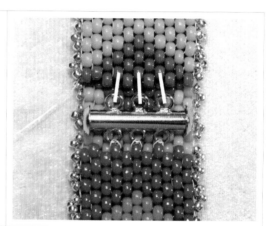

3. Start moving to the first connection point by going UP through the bead next to the thread.

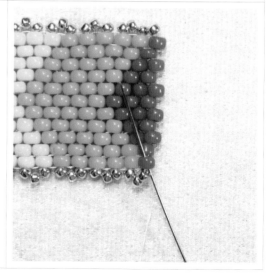

4. Continue moving up one bead at a time.

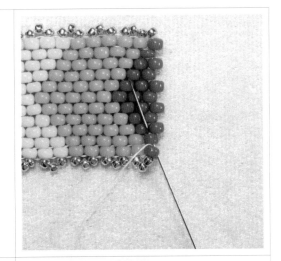

5. Move up one more bead and you are in position to start adding your clasp.

6. Fold your beadwork over so the clasp is next to the other end of the bracelet. Obviously you don't want to twist the bracelet. Make sure it's flat.
7. Run your needle through the first loop of the clasp.

8. Run your needle through the next "up" bead, skipping the "down" bead.

9. Run your needle through the next loop on the clasp.

10. Run your needle through the next "up" bead (again skipping the down bead).
11. Repeat Steps 9 and 10 for the remaining loop on the clasp.

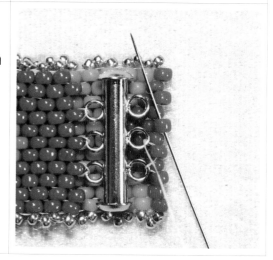

12. Run your needle back through beads to get to
    the last loop you connected.

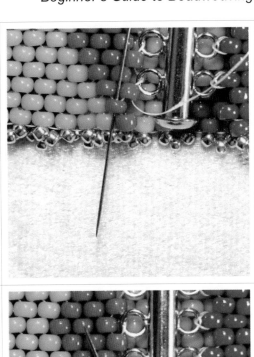

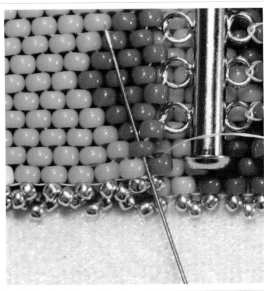

13. Run your needle back through the loops and beads the same way you did on the other end to anchor the clasp firmly.
14. Run your needle down through several beads to weave the thread in solidly.
15. Trim your thread.

Congratulations! Your bracelet is finished!

Project Pattern

Chevrons

Page 1

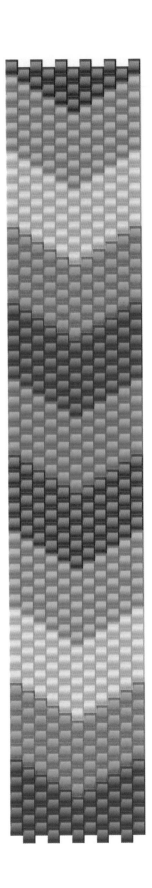

☐ Chart #:A
8-404
Opaque Yellow
Count:110

☐ Chart #:B
8-406
Opaque Orange
Count:110

☐ Chart #:C
8-411
Opaque Jade Green
Count:76

☐ Chart #:D
8-413
Opaque Turquoise Blue
Count:55

☐ Chart #:E
8-416
Opaque Chartreuse
Count:110

☐ Chart #:F
8-1477
Opaque Purple
Count:100

Row 1&2 (L) (11)C

Row 3 (R) (1)E, (4)C, (1)E

Row 4 (L) (1)E, (3)C, (1)E

Row 5 (R) (2)E, (2)C, (2)E

Row 6 (L) (2)E, (1)C, (2)E

Row 7 (R) (6)E

Row 8 (L) (5)E

Row 9 (R) (6)E

Row 10 (L) (5)E

Row 11 (R) (6)E

Row 12 (L) (5)E

Row 13 (R) (1)A, (4)E, (1)A

Row 14 (L) (1)A, (3)E, (1)A

Row 15 (R) (2)A, (2)E, (2)A

Row 16 (L) (2)A, (1)E, (2)A

Row 17 (R) (6)A

Row 18 (L) (5)A

Row 19 (R) (6)A

Row 20 (L) (5)A

Row 21 (R) (6)A

Row 22 (L) (5)A

Row 23 (R) (1)B, (4)A, (1)B

Row 24 (L) (1)B, (3)A, (1)B

Row 25 (R) (2)B, (2)A, (2)B

Row 26 (L) (2)B, (1)A, (2)B

Row 27 (R) (6)B

Row 28 (L) (5)B

Row 29 (R) (6)B

Row 30 (L) (5)B

Row 31 (R) (6)B

Row 32 (L) (5)B

Row 33 (R) (1)F, (4)B, (1)F

Row 34 (L) (1)F, (3)B, (1)F

Row 35 (R) (2)F, (2)B, (2)F

Row 36 (L) (2)F, (1)B, (2)F

Row 37 (R) (6)F

Row 38 (L) (5)F

Row 39 (R) (6)F

Row 40 (L) (5)F

Row 41 (R) (6)F

Row 42 (L) (5)F

Row 43 (R) (1)D, (4)F, (1)D

Row 44 (L) (1)D, (3)F, (1)D

Row 45 (R) (2)D, (2)F, (2)D

Row 46 (L) (2)D, (1)F, (2)D

Row 47 (R) (6)D

Row 48 (L) (5)D

Row 49 (R) (6)D

Row 50 (L) (5)D

Row 51 (R) (6)D

Row 52 (L) (5)D

Row 53 (R) (1)C, (4)D, (1)C

Row 54 (L) (1)C, (3)D, (1)C

Row 55 (R) (2)C, (2)D, (2)C

Row 56 (L) (2)C, (1)D, (2)C

Row 57 (R) (6)C

Row 58 (L) (5)C

Row 59 (R) (6)C

Row 60 (L) (5)C

Row 61 (R) (6)C

Row 62 (L) (5)C

Row 63 (R) (1)E, (4)C, (1)E

Row 64 (L) (1)E, (3)C, (1)E

Row 65 (R) (2)E, (2)C, (2)E

Row 66 (L) (2)E, (1)C, (2)E

Row 67 (R) (6)E

Row 68 (L) (5)E

Row 69 (R) (6)E

Row 70 (L) (5)E

Row 71 (R) (6)E

Chevrons

Row 72 (L) (5)E
Row 73 (R) (1)A, (4)E, (1)A
Row 74 (L) (1)A, (3)E, (1)A
Row 75 (R) (2)A, (2)E, (2)A
Row 76 (L) (2)A, (1)E, (2)A
Row 77 (R) (6)A
Row 78 (L) (5)A
Row 79 (R) (6)A
Row 80 (L) (5)A
Row 81 (R) (6)A
Row 82 (L) (5)A
Row 83 (R) (1)B, (4)A, (1)B
Row 84 (L) (1)B, (3)A, (1)B
Row 85 (R) (2)B, (2)A, (2)B
Row 86 (L) (2)B, (1)A, (2)B
Row 87 (R) (6)B
Row 88 (L) (5)B
Row 89 (R) (6)B
Row 90 (L) (5)B
Row 91 (R) (6)B
Row 92 (L) (5)B
Row 93 (R) (1)F, (4)B, (1)F
Row 94 (L) (1)F, (3)B, (1)F
Row 95 (R) (2)F, (2)B, (2)F
Row 96 (L) (2)F, (1)B, (2)F
Row 97 (R) (6)F
Row 98 (L) (5)F
Row 99 (R) (6)F
Row 100 (L) (5)F
Row 101 (R) (6)F
Row 102 (L) (5)F

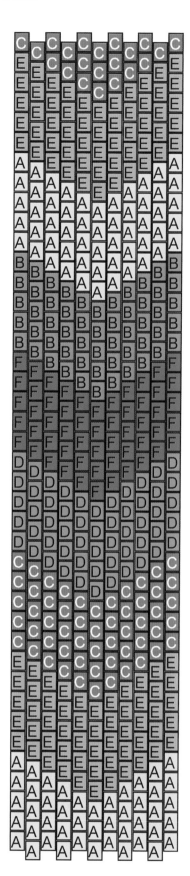

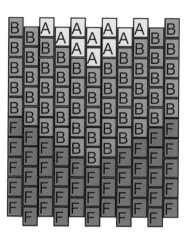

2-Drop Peyote

Multi-drop peyote (2-drop, 3-drop, etc.) is a great stitch for quick beading. It is exactly the same as single-drop peyote except that you pick up 2 beads instead of 1 and you go through 2 beads instead of 1. This tutorial is not a project, but instead you will create practice swatches to get familiar with 2-drop peyote, even and odd count.

Peyote Stitch	How Many Beads Per Row Even Count	How Many Bead Per Row Odd Count
2-Drop	Multiple of 4 (4, 8, 12, etc.)	Multiple of 4 plus 2 (6, 10, 14, etc.)
3-Drop	Multiple of 6 (6, 12, 18, etc.)	Multiple of 6 plus 3 (9, 15, 21, etc.)

Table of Contents

2-Drop Peyote — Even Count

1. Pick up 12 beads.	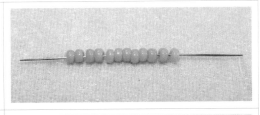
2. Pick up 2 more beads, skip the first 2 beads, and go through the next 2 beads.	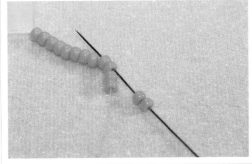

3. You may need to nudge the beads a bit and then your work should look like this.

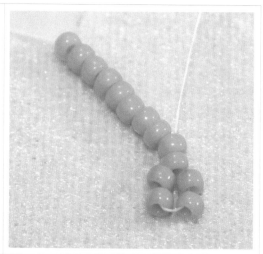

4. Pick up 2 more beads, skip the next two beads after the thread, and go through the next 2 beads.

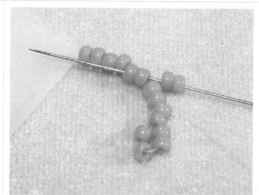

5. Again, some nudging may be necessary and your work will look like this.

6. Repeat step 4 one more time. Then your work will look like this.

7. Turn your work around. Pick up 2 beads, skip the first 2 beads, and go through the next 2 beads.

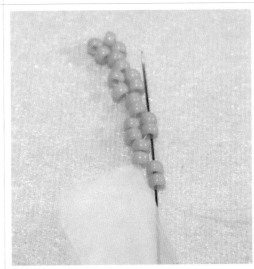

8. Repeat.

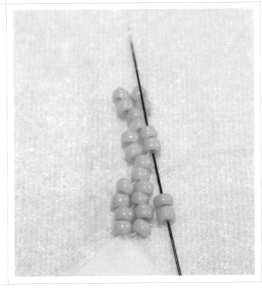

9. Repeat again and your work looks like this at the end of the row.

10. Repeat until you have finished all the rows in your pattern.

2-Drop Peyote — Odd Count

1. Pick up 14 beads.

2. Pick up 2 more beads, skip the first 2 beads, and go through the next 2 beads.

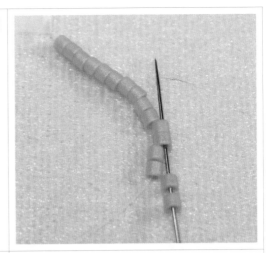

3. You may need to nudge the beads a bit and then your work should look like this.

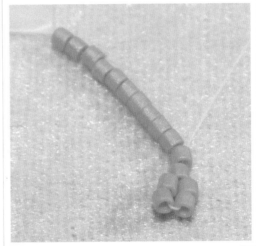

4. Pick up 2 more beads, skip the next two beads after the thread, and go through the next 2 beads.

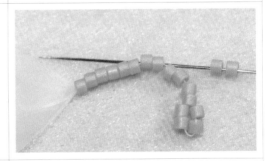

5. Again, some nudging may be necessary and your work will look like this.

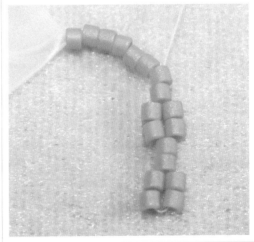

6. Repeat step 4 one more time. Then your work will look like this.

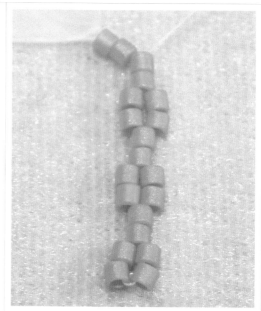

7. Now you need to add 2 more beads but there is nowhere to go after the beads, right? This is the odd count turn. The goal is to add those 2 odd beads and get the needle back into position to start the next row.

   Pick up 2 beads and needle DOWN through the top 2 beads. Really.

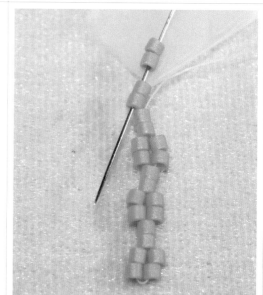

8. You may need to nudge the beads into place. Your work will now look like this, with the thread coming out of the top 2 beads, facing down.

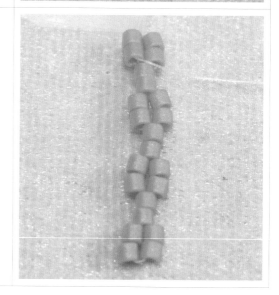

9. Run your needle DOWN through the next 2 beads.

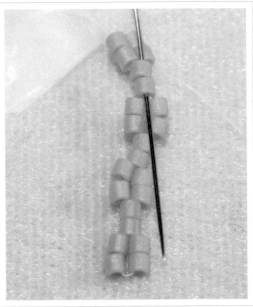

10. Run your needle DOWN through the next 2 beads on the right.

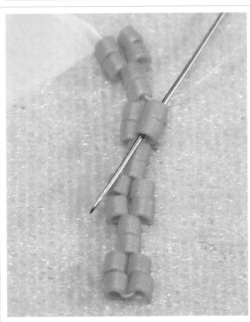

11. Run your needle UP through the 2 beads on the left.

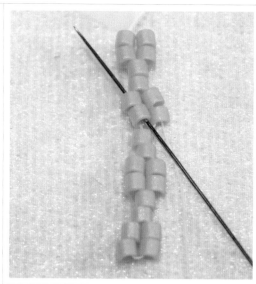

12. Run your needle UP through the next 2 beads above the current position.

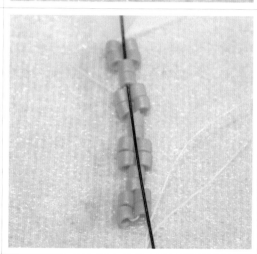

13. Run your needle UP through the top 2 beads on the left.

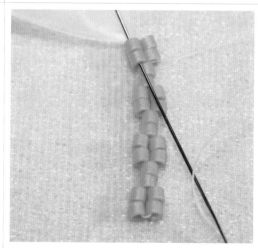

14. Run your needle DOWN through the 2 beads on the right. You are finally back in position to start the next row. Whew! It will get easier, trust me.

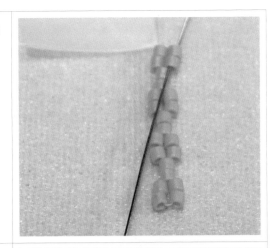

15. Turn your work around. Pick up 2 beads, skip the first 2 beads, and go through the next 2 beads.

    Continue picking up 2 beads, skipping the next 2 beads, and going through the next 2 beads until you are the end of the row.

    This is an EVEN row.

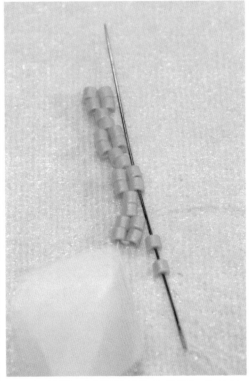

16. Turn your work over and start the next row.

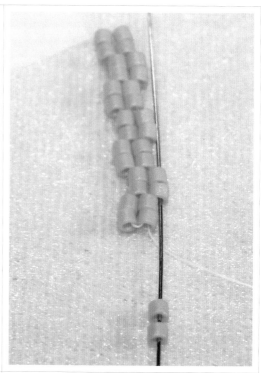

17. When you get to the last 2 beads in the row, pick up 2 beads, and needle DOWN through the 6 beads on the right. This is combining 3 steps we did at the beginning. It's easier to do this now that we have a base to work with.

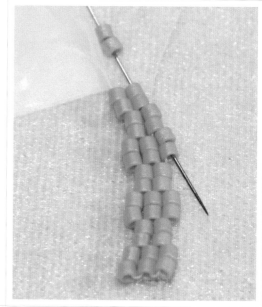

18. Needle UP through the 2 beads to the left of the current thread position.

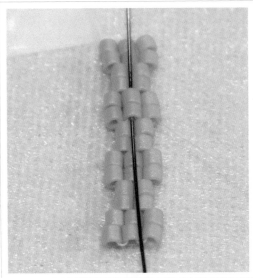

19. Needle UP through the 2 beads above and to the right of the current thread position.

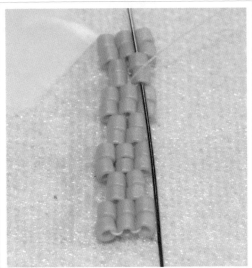

20. Needle UP through the 2 beads above and to the left of the current thread position.

   If it's comfortable for you, you can combine steps 19 and 20 and needle up through 4 beads at once.

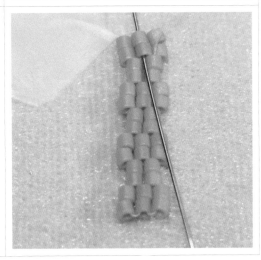

21. Needle DOWN through the 2 beads on the right. This completes the ODD row.

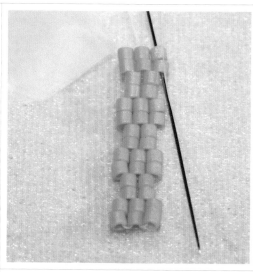

22. Repeat until you have finished all the rows in your pattern. This photo is turned 90 degrees.

Brick Stitch for Shaped Beadwork

Brick stitch allows you to make increases and decreases within a project with relative ease. In this tutorial, we will brick stitch this heart, shown on the left as peyote stitch and on the right as brick stitch. The only difference in the images is that the one on the right is turned 90 degrees. (Image is from Shala Kerrigan at http://www.bellaonline.com/about/beadwork.)

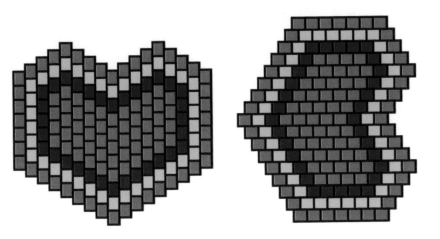

Table of Contents

Prepare Your Pattern

1. Print out the pattern. It's much easier to follow if you can place a ruler on the row you are currently beading.

2. Find the widest part of the pattern. It is often, but not always, the center. In this case, there is no obvious widest part so we will start at the center. The line shows the first row we will bead.

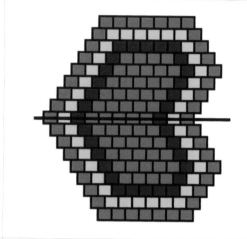

3. I wrote row numbers on the diagram to make it easier to follow. I alternated left and right since that is the direction you will be beading.

4. I then turned the diagram 180 degrees and wrote the row numbers on the other side, in the order in which we will be beading.

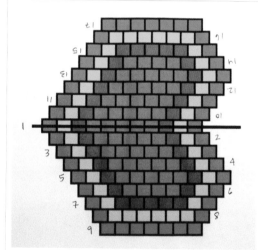

Bead First Row - Ladder Stitch

1. I like to lay out the beads for each row before I start beading it. Here are the beads for the first row.

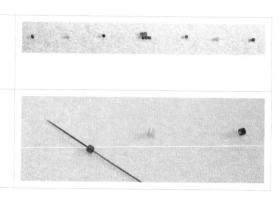

2. Pick up the first bead for row 1.

3. Pick up the second bead for row 1.

4. Run the needle UP through the first bead you picked up.

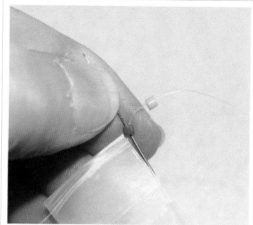

5. Run the needle DOWN through the second bead you picked up. This is the start of ladder stitch, which we will be using for the first row.

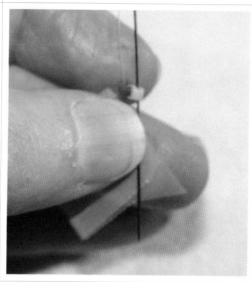

6. Pick up the third bead for row 1 and needle DOWN through the previous bead.

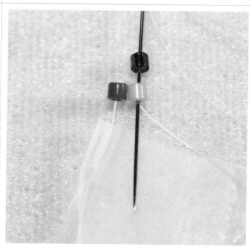

7. Make sure the new bead is settled next to the previous bead and needle UP through the bead you just added.

8. Pick up the next bead and needle UP through the previous bead.

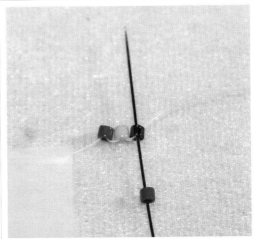

9. Settle the new bead in place and needle DOWN through the new bead.

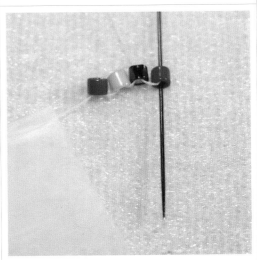

10. Continue adding beads as in steps 6 through 9 until you have the entire first row done.

Second Row - Brick Stitch Starting with an "Outie"

I look at the diagram to determine if the first bead is an "innie" or "outie" (my terms).
For example:

- The first bead of row 2 is an "outie" relative to the last bead of row 1 because it sticks out beyond the end of the last bead of row 1.
- The first bead of row 3 is an "innie" relative to the last bead of row 2 because it is "inside" the width of the last bead of row 2.

Every brick stitch row starts by picking up 2 beads (unless the whole row only has 1 bead).

- If the new bead is an "outie", then you go under the first thread bridge you have available after you pick up the 2 new beads.
- If the new bead is an "innie", then you need to reposition your thread to go under the second thread bridge.

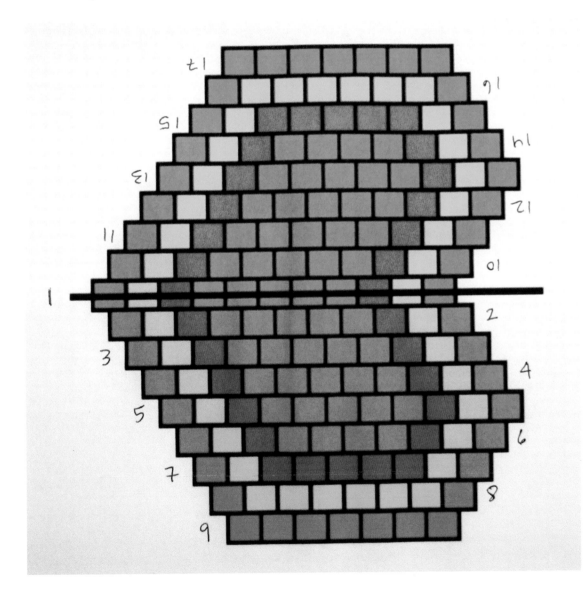

1. Move your ruler to just below the edge of row 2.

2. Pick up the beads for row 2, starting on the right side since that is where you will start beading.

3. Pick up the first 2 beads for row 2.
   Since this is an "outie" row, run your needle below the first thread bridge of row 1, in between the first 2 beads of row 1.

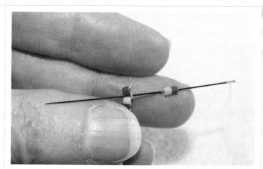

4. If necessary, nudge the beads in place so the new beads are aligned as in this photo.

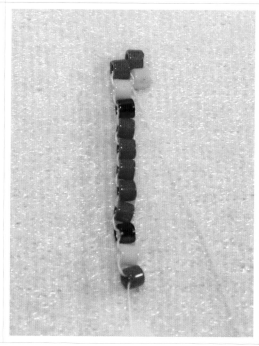

5. Run your needle UP through the second bead of the 2 you just added.

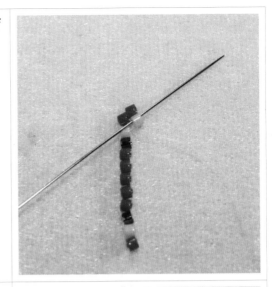

6. Your beads will look like this with the thread coming up out of the second new bead, ready to pick up your next bead.

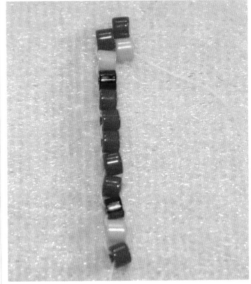

7. Pick up a single bead and run your needle under the next thread bridge, between the second and third beads of the first row.

8. Run your needle UP through the bead you just added.

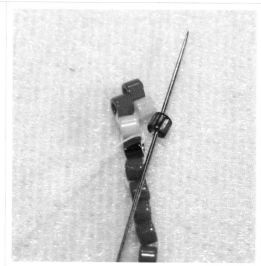

9. Continue adding single beads for the rest of the row, as in steps 7 and 8. Your work will look like this.

Third Row - Brick Stitch Starting with an "Innie"

1. Move your ruler to just below the edge of row 3.

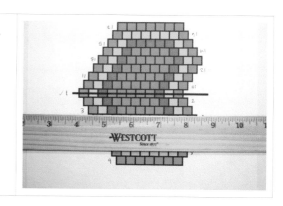

2. Pick up the beads for row 3, starting on the right side since that is where you will start beading.

3. Look at the bead chart. You will see that this is an "innie" row. We need to position our needle over one thread bridge to get in the correct position to add the "innie" beads. To start this process, run your needle under the first thread bridge.

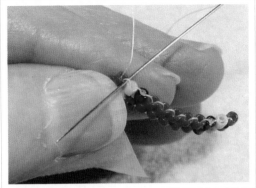

4. Next run your needle DOWN through the first bead in the previous row.

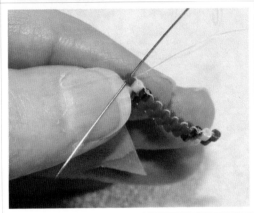

5. Next run your needle UP through the second bead in the previous row.

6. You are now in position to add the "innie" beads. Pick up the first 2 beads of row 3 and run your needle under the thread bridge between beads 2 and 3 of the previous row.

7. Nudge your beads into position and run your needle UP through the last bead you just added.

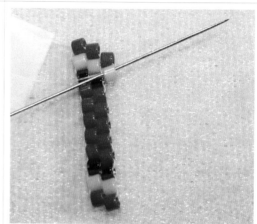

8. Add the rest of the beads except for the last one for this row, using the same technique as in steps 6 and 7 but only add 1 bead at a time. Remember you only add 2 beads at the beginning of a new row.

9. Now we have a new problem. There is no thread bridge at the end of the row for the last bead. So, we will use ladder stitch to add it. Pick up a bead and run your needle back UP through the previous bead.

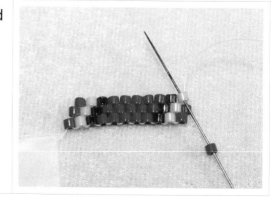

10. This is how your work will look at the end of the third row.

Rest of the Rows

Next you need to position your needle properly to add the next row.

Because you had to add the last bead using ladder stitch, your thread is coming out of the second to last bead. When you turn your work around, this would be perfect if the next row started with an "innie" bead.

However, the next row starts with an "outie" bead so we need to navigate so the thread is coming out of the last bead.

1. Go under the thread bridge to the left of the bead the thread is coming out of.

2. Pull the thread through and go DOWN through the second to last bead in the row.

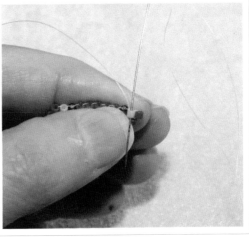

3. Go UP through the last bead in the row. You are now ready to start beading like you did for the second row, an "outie" row.

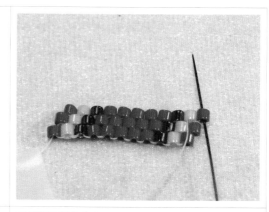

4. When you finish the first half of this project, it will look like this.

5. Next we need to get to the starting point for the second half. Go under the thread bridge to the left of the current position.

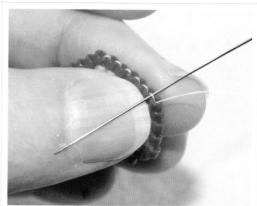

6. Go DOWN through the last bead in the row.

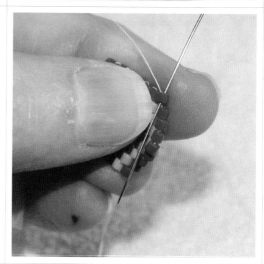

7. Go DOWN through the rest of the beads along this edge. If there are "innies" and "outies", go through each bead individually until you get to the end of the edge.

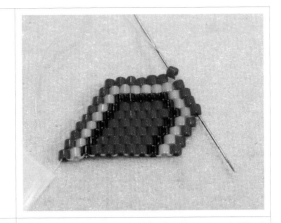

8. In this case, there is one more section in line to go through.

9. When you get to the bottom of the first half, turn your pattern 180 degrees so you are ready to start the second half.
10. Continue beading additional rows, noting whether each is an "innie" or an "outie".

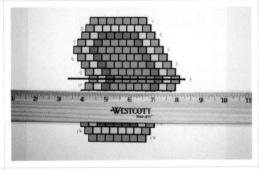

11. When you finish all the rows, run your thread and your tail through the outer edge beads like you did in steps 7 and 8.

Square Stitch Bracelet

In this tutorial, I describe the steps to make a bracelet using *square stitch*. In square stitch, beads line up in straight lines, vertically and horizontally, in the same way as they do on a loom. Because of this, you can use square stitch to bead pieces that were designed for a loom.

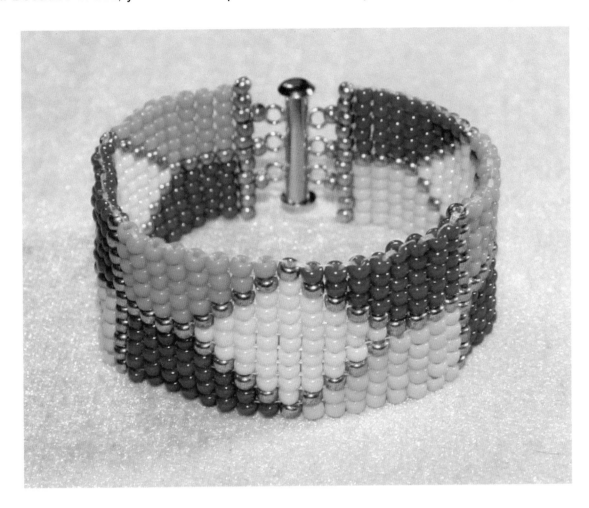

Table of Contents

Supplies

This bracelet is going to be 11 columns wide by 55 rows long. A word chart and bead chart are provided with this tutorial for you to follow while beading. The pattern also includes bead counts for each color. You can use any colors you like, of course. You will need:

- **Beads**: *8/0 seed beads*
  - Color A - 3.5 grams
  - Color B - 2.5 grams
  - Color C - 4.5 grams
  - Color D - 2.5 grams
  - Color E - 3.5 grams
- **Clasp:** any clasp the same width or narrower than the finished beadwork; we are using a 3-strand slide clasp for this tutorial
- **Thread**: FireLine 6lb thread (crystal)

1 Prepare Your Work Area

Assemble the tools you need for this project.

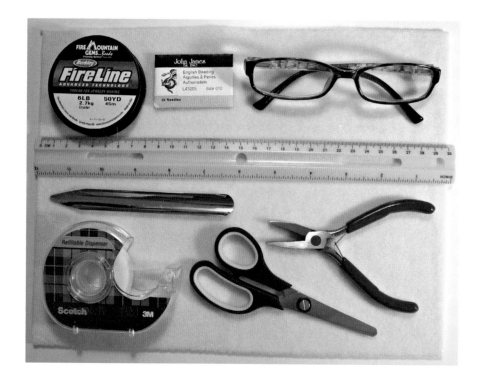

Line up the beads for this project, in the order you plan to use them, and put a tag next to each color with a letter.

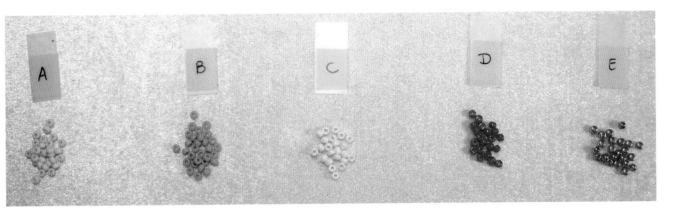

2 Bead the First Two Rows

1. Thread your needle. I use tape in place of a stop bead about 10 inches from the end of the thread.	
2. I usually lay out the beads for each row, in order. In this case, the first row is all the same color so pick up 11 "E" beads and pull them down to the tape.	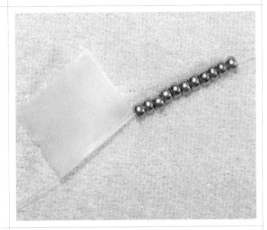
3. Lay out the beads for the second row.	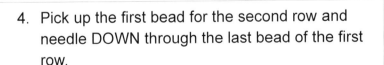
4. Pick up the first bead for the second row and needle DOWN through the last bead of the first row.	

5. Needle UP through the bead you just added. This puts your needle in position to add the next bead and anchors the bead you just added.

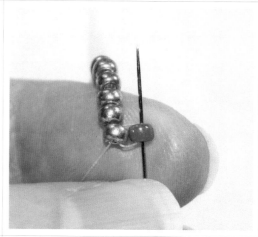

6. Pick up the second bead for the row and needle DOWN through JUST the bead next to it, the next to last bead of the first row.

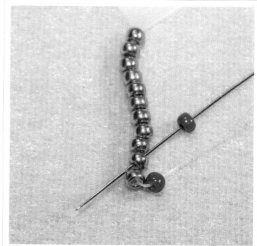

7. Needle UP through ONLY the bead you just added.

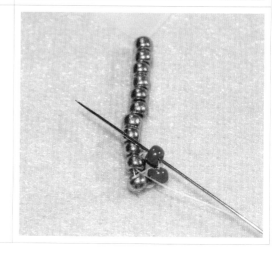

8. Your beadwork should now look like this.

9. Continue to add beads as in steps 7 through 9 until you have added all 11 beads for row 2 of your bracelet.

10. Flip your work over so the thread is coming out of the bottom of the beadwork.

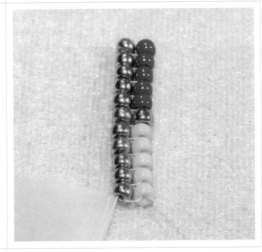

11. Run your needle UP through the first row of beads.

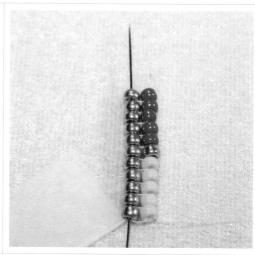

12. Run your needle DOWN through the second row of beads.

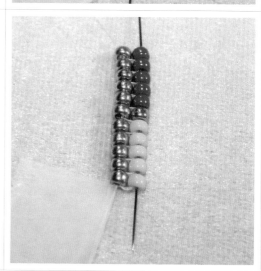

3 Bead Row Number 3 and Beyond

1. Lay out the beads for row 3.

2. Flip your work so the thread is coming out of the bottom.
3. Pick up the first bead for row 3 and run your needle DOWN through the bead to the left of where the thread is coming out the last bead of the previous row.

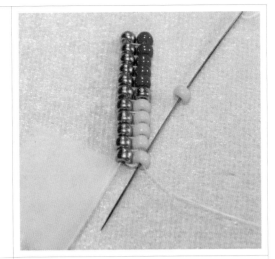

4. Run your needle UP through the bead you just added.

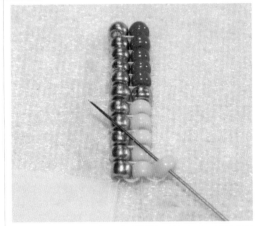

5. Pick up the next bead and run your needle DOWN through JUST the bead to its left, the second to last bead in the previous row.

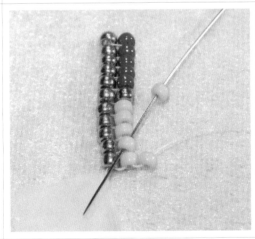

6. Run your needle back UP through the bead you just added.	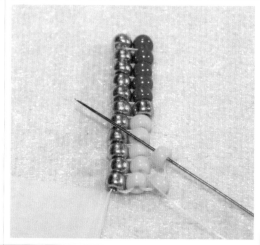
7. When you finish this row, your work will look like this.	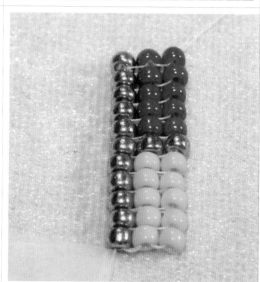
8. Repeat the steps in this section until you have completed all 55 rows for the pattern. See the next section for what to do when you need to add thread.	

4 Add Thread

There are a number of methods for adding thread during a project. The method I use for square stitch projects uses a square knot (how appropriate!) and melted thread ends. This allows you to pull the threads so you just end up with a small "blob" join. There are a number of video tutorials that show how to do this and I recommend them since it's easier to see than with a photo tutorial. Go to youtube.com and search for "FireLine join" and you will find them.

Note that this method only works for thread that melts into a blob on the end, such as FireLine. If you are using a thread that does not melt on the end, use one of the knotting techniques, such as the one I describe in my *Absolute Beginner's Guide to Beadweaving - Peyote Bracelet* tutorial.

5 Add Your Clasp - Part 1

We are going to use a 3-strand slide clasp, which looks like this. The narrow end of the clasp slides into the wider end of the clasp when worn. Slide your clasp together now to start adding it to your bracelet.

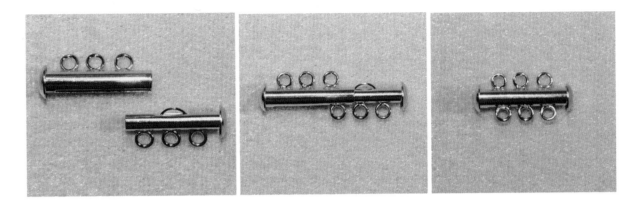

1. Turn your work and run your needle UP through the second row of your work, next to the bead where the thread is coming out.

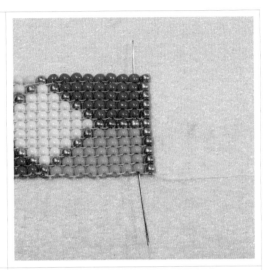

2. Run your needle UP through the first 3 beads of the last row.

Beginner's Guide to Beadweaving

3. Pick up 1 gold bead and run your needle up through one of the end loops of one side of the clasp.

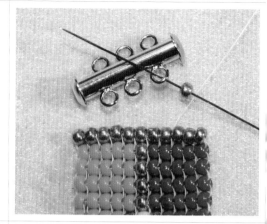

4. Pull your clasp down to your work and it will look like this.

5. Run your needle DOWN through the gold bead you just added. Make sure you don't back out through the loop.

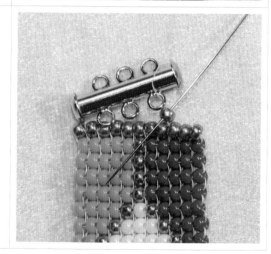

6. Run your needle UP through the next 3 beads in the row.

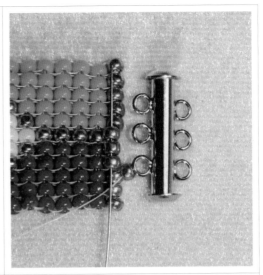

7. Pick up another gold bead and run your needle UP through the next loop in the clasp.

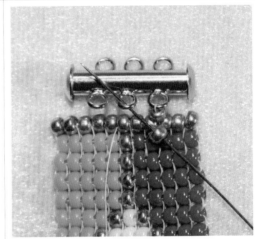

8. Run your needle back DOWN through the bead you just added to the clasp.

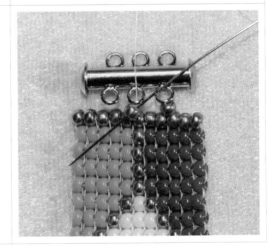

9. Repeat steps 6 through 8 to add the last bead to the last clasp loop.
10. Run your needle UP through the last 2 beads in the row (yes, 2 beads this time instead of 3).

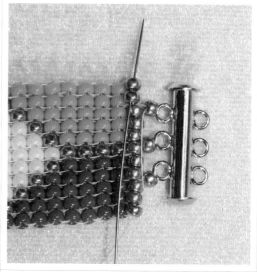

11. Run your needle up through the thread bridge and go back through the beads and loops to reinforce the stitches.
12. Trim your thread.

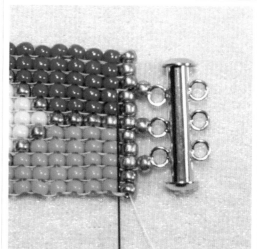

6 Reinforce Your Rows

Once you have added the clasp to the first end of your bracelet, we will go back through all the rows to reinforce them. This will give your bracelet more body and will make the stitching more secure.

1. Run your needle UP through the row next to where your thread is coming out.

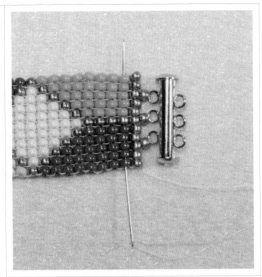

2. Flip your work so the thread is coming out of the bottom.
3. Run your UP through the row next to where your thread is coming out.
4. Continue flipping and going through the next row until you get to the other end of your bracelet.

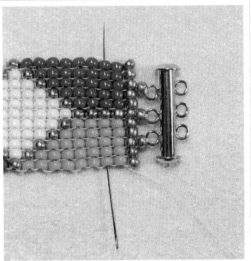

Notes:
- Don't pull through too hard or you will distort your beadwork.
- Make sure you go through every bead, not over or under any bead.

7 Add Your Clasp - Part 2

1. If you haven't already done so, remove the tape from your tail thread on the other end of your beadwork and put your needle on the thread.
2. Weave your tail thread through the rows using the same method you did to reinforce your beadwork.
3. Trim your tail thread, without cutting any other threads.

4. Run your needle up through the thread bridge between the first two rows of beadwork and pull through.

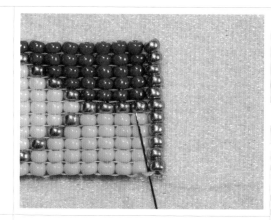

5. Go UP through the first 3 beads of the last row.

6. Fold the other end over so the clasp is near the end you are working on.
7. Pick up a bead and go up through the first loop of the clasp, as you did in the last section.

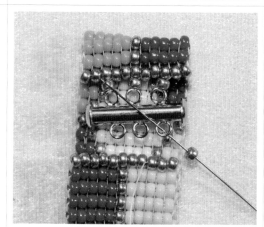

8. Go back down through the bead you just added, as you did in the last section.

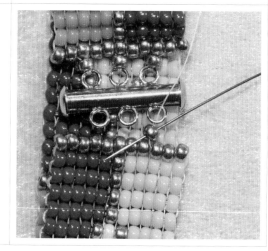

9. Go through the next 3 beads and repeat the rest of the steps you did in the previous section to go through the other loops AND to go back and reinforce your stitching through all the loops on this end of the clasp.

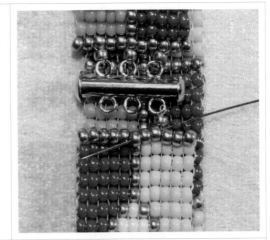

10. Your bracelet is finished!

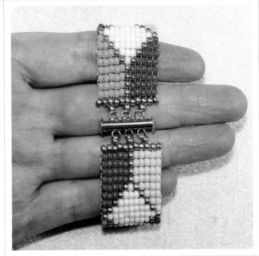

Congratulations! Your square stitch bracelet is finished!

Project Pattern

Quilt Block Pattern v3 - Square Stitch

Chart #:A
8-404
Opaque Yellow
Count:90

Chart #:B
8-416
Opaque Chartreuse
Count:90

Chart #:C
8-594
Cream Ceylon
Count:123

Chart #:D
8-1477
Opaque Purple
Count:180

Chart #:E
8-4202
Galvanized Gold
Count:122

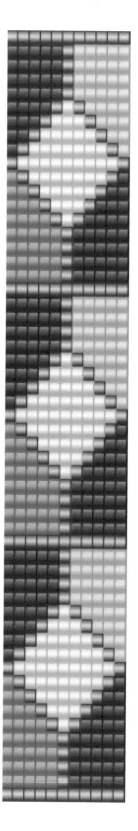

Quilt Block Pattern v3 - Square Stitch

Row 1 (L) (11)E
Row 2 (R) (5)D, (1)E, (5)A
Row 3 (L) (5)A, (1)E, (5)D
Row 4 (R) (5)D, (1)E, (5)A
Row 5 (L) (5)A, (1)E, (5)D
Row 6 (R) (4)D, (1)E, (1)C, (1)E, (4)A
Row 7 (L) (3)A, (1)E, (3)C, (1)E, (3)D
Row 8 (R) (2)D, (1)E, (5)C, (1)E, (2)A
Row 9 (L) (1)A, (1)E, (7)C, (1)E, (1)D
Row 10 (R) (1)E, (9)C, (1)E
Row 11 (L) (1)D, (1)E, (7)C, (1)E, (1)B
Row 12 (R) (2)B, (1)E, (5)C, (1)E, (2)D
Row 13 (L) (3)D, (1)E, (3)C, (1)E, (3)B
Row 14 (R) (4)B, (1)E, (1)C, (1)E, (4)D
Row 15 (L) (5)D, (1)E, (5)B
Row 16 (R) (5)B, (1)E, (5)D
Row 17 (L) (5)D, (1)E, (5)B
Row 18 (R) (5)B, (1)E, (5)D
Row 19 (L) (11)E
Row 20 (R) (5)D, (1)E, (5)A
Row 21 (L) (5)A, (1)E, (5)D
Row 22 (R) (5)D, (1)E, (5)A
Row 23 (L) (5)A, (1)E, (5)D
Row 24 (R) (4)D, (1)E, (1)C, (1)E, (4)A
Row 25 (L) (3)A, (1)E, (3)C, (1)E, (3)D
Row 26 (R) (2)D, (1)E, (5)C, (1)E, (2)A
Row 27 (L) (1)A, (1)E, (7)C, (1)E, (1)D
Row 28 (R) (1)E, (9)C, (1)E
Row 29 (L) (1)D, (1)E, (7)C, (1)E, (1)B
Row 30 (R) (2)B, (1)E, (5)C, (1)E, (2)D
Row 31 (L) (3)D, (1)E, (3)C, (1)E, (3)B
Row 32 (R) (4)B, (1)E, (1)C, (1)E, (4)D
Row 33 (L) (5)D, (1)E, (5)B
Row 34 (R) (5)B, (1)E, (5)D
Row 35 (L) (5)D, (1)E, (5)B

Row 36 (R) (5)B, (1)E, (5)D
Row 37 (L) (11)E
Row 38 (R) (5)D, (1)E, (5)A
Row 39 (L) (5)A, (1)E, (5)D
Row 40 (R) (5)D, (1)E, (5)A
Row 41 (L) (5)A, (1)E, (5)D
Row 42 (R) (4)D, (1)E, (1)C, (1)E, (4)A
Row 43 (L) (3)A, (1)E, (3)C, (1)E, (3)D
Row 44 (R) (2)D, (1)E, (5)C, (1)E, (2)A
Row 45 (L) (1)A, (1)E, (7)C, (1)E, (1)D
Row 46 (R) (1)E, (9)C, (1)E
Row 47 (L) (1)D, (1)E, (7)C, (1)E, (1)B
Row 48 (R) (2)B, (1)E, (5)C, (1)E, (2)D
Row 49 (L) (3)D, (1)E, (3)C, (1)E, (3)B
Row 50 (R) (4)B, (1)E, (1)C, (1)E, (4)D
Row 51 (L) (5)D, (1)E, (5)B
Row 52 (R) (5)B, (1)E, (5)D
Row 53 (L) (5)D, (1)E, (5)B
Row 54 (R) (5)B, (1)E, (5)D
Row 55 (L) (11)E

Quilt Block Pattern v3 - Square Stitch

Herringbone Bracelet

In this tutorial, I describe the steps to make a bracelet using the beadweaving stitch called *herringbone*. In herringbone stitch, beads are added two at a time and each pair of beads slants inward slightly. This gives the beadwork an interesting texture and many different kinds of beads can be used.

Table of Contents

Supplies

This bracelet is going to be 10 columns wide by about 60 rows long. It will use 5 different colors of size 8/0 seed beads, like this. We will call the colors A through E, with A on the left and E on the right. You will also be adding size 11/0 seed beads along the edges.

- **Beads**: *8/0 seed beads*
  - Color A - 4 grams (Miyuki 8-421)
  - Color B - 4 grams (Miyuki 8-404)
  - Color C - 4 grams (Miyuki 8-4202)
  - Color D - 4 grams (Miyuki 8-416)
  - Color E - 4 grams (Miyuki 8-417L)
- **Beads:** *11/0 seed beads - 1.5 grams (Miyuki 11-4202)*
- **Clasp:** any clasp the same width or narrower than the finished beadwork; we are using a 5-strand slide clasp for this tutorial
- **Thread**: FireLine 6lb thread (crystal)

1 Prepare Your Work Area

Assemble the tools you need for this project.

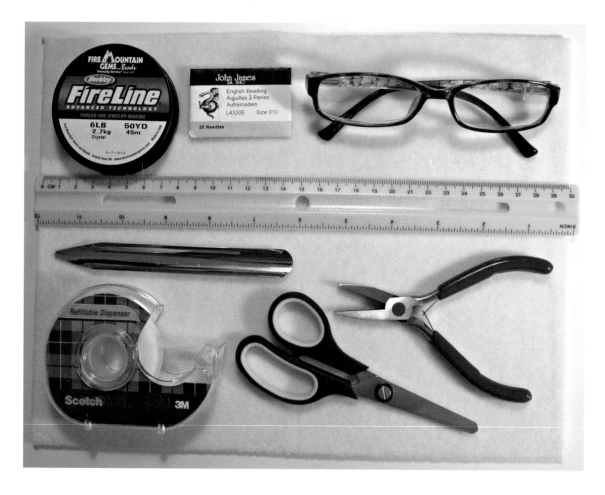

Line up the beads for this project, in the order you plan to use them, and put a tag next to each color with a letter.

2 Start Your First Two Rows

To prepare for your herringbone bracelet, you first create a base using *ladder* stitch.

1. Thread your needle. I use tape in place of a stop bead about 10 inches from the end of the thread. 2. Lay out the beads for your first two rows, in this order: AAAA BBBB CCCC DDDD EEEE	
3. Pick up the first 4 beads in the line and bring them down to the tape.	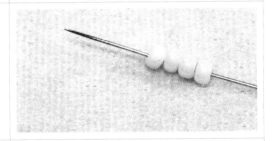
4. Run your needle UP through the first 2 of the 4 beads, allowing the second 2 beads to come down to the right, next to the first 2 beads.	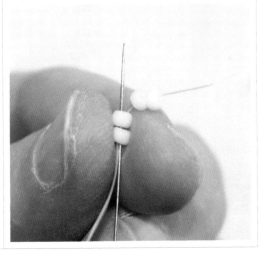

5. Run your needle DOWN through the 2 beads on the right.

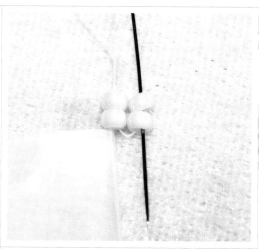

6. Pick up the next 2 beads in line (the first beads of the second color) and run your needle DOWN through the previous beads.

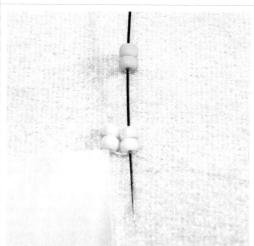

7. Run your needle UP through the beads you just added.

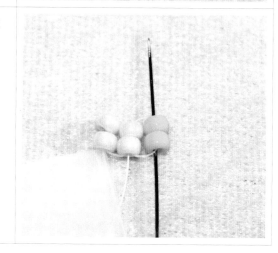

8. Pick up the next 2 beads in line (the third and fourth beads of the second color) and run your needle UP through the previous beads.

Important: At this point, notice that when you are adding a bead, you are always running your needle through the opposite end of the bead where the thread is coming out.

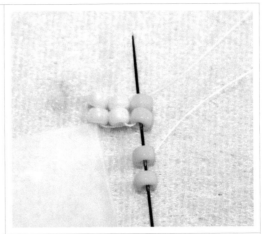

9. Run your needle DOWN through the beads you just added.
10. Continue to add beads as in Steps 6 through 9 until you have added all 20 beads for rows 1 and 2 of your bracelet.

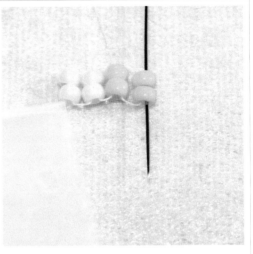

Important: At this point, notice that on the step after you add beads, you are going down or up through the new beads, depending on which direction the thread is coming out of the previous beads. If the thread is coming up out of the previous beads, you run your needle down through the new beads, and vice versa.

11. Your first two rows should look like this when you are done adding all the beads.

3 Bead Row Number 3

Now we get to start adding rows using herringbone stitch!

1. Lay out the beads for row 3, in the reverse order as you did for rows 1 and 2: EE DD CC BB AA	
2. Turn your beadwork so the working thread is coming out on the left. 3. Pick up the first two beads for row 2. You always pick up two beads at a time for herringbone. 4. Run your needle DOWN through the 2 beads to the right of where the thread is coming out.	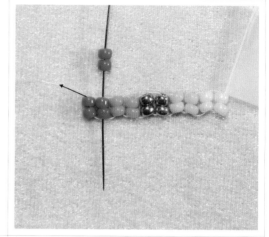
5. Run your needle UP through the 2 beads to the right of where your thread is coming out. **Note**: You may need to give the newly-added beads a nudge to make sure their holes are pointing up and towards each other.	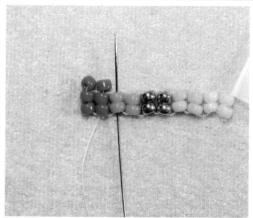
6. Pick up the next two beads in line. 7. Run your needle DOWN through the 2 beads on the right of where your thread is coming out.	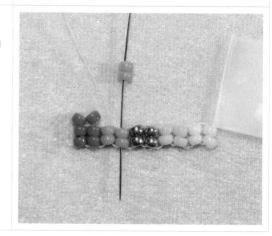

8. Run your needle UP through the 2 beads to the right of where your thread is coming out.

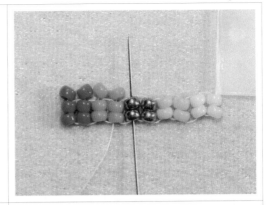

9. Repeat Steps 6 through 8 until you have used all the beads for the row.
   On the last set of beads, only go DOWN through ONE bead instead of two.

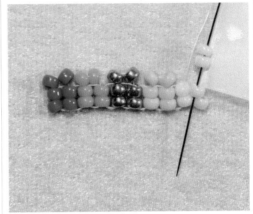

10. Your beadwork should look like this when you finish adding the beads for the row.

11. At the end of the row, you want to hide the thread that would show if you just ran your needle up to the next row, so you do what we call a *turnaround*.
12. Pick up two 11/0 seed beads.
13. Run your needle UP through the bead above the bead where the thread is coming out.

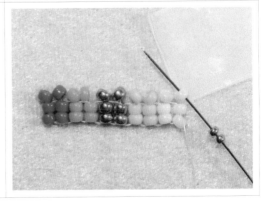

14. Your work should look this this after adding the turnaround beads.

4 Bead Additional Rows

1. Lay out the beads back in the original order:
   AA BB CC DD EE

2. Turn your beadwork so the working thread is coming out on the left.
3. Pick up the first two beads for row 3.
4. Run your needle DOWN through the bead next to the bead where your thread is coming out, making sure that you do **not** go through the bottom 2 beads.

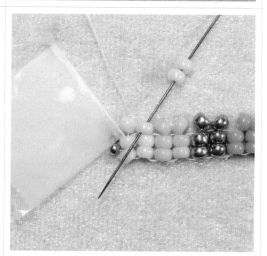

5. Run your needle UP through the next bead to the right.

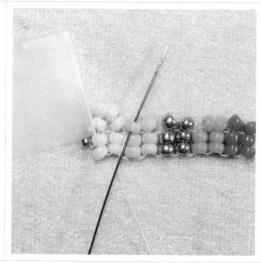

6. Pick up the next two beads.
7. Run your needle down through the bead next to the bead where your thread is coming out, making sure that you do **not** go through the bottom 2 beads.

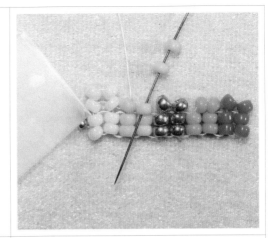

8. Run your needle UP through the next bead to the right.

9. Repeat Steps 6 through 8 until you reach the end of the row.
10. Pick up two 11/0 seed beads.
11. Run your needle up through the bead above the bead where the thread is coming out.

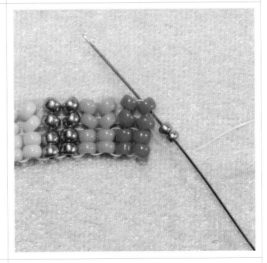

12. Repeat the steps in this section until your beadwork is 6 inches long. This will make a small bracelet. If you want a longer bracelet, add more rows.
13. At some point you will need to add thread. Follow the steps in the next section for

instructions on how to do that.

14. When your beadwork is 6 inches long, go to section 6 to start adding your clasp.

5 Add Thread

There are a number of methods for adding thread during a project. This is the method I use for herringbone stitch projects, which is slightly different from the method I use for adding thread for peyote stitch projects.

1. Pick a location near but not at the beginning of a row, so the knot will be hidden in the beading and will not show on the edge. 2. Pull a length of thread to match the length between your outstretched arms and cut from the spool. 3. Line up the end of the new thread with the end of the old thread.	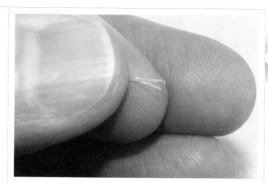
4. Run your fingers down to the end by your beadwork, keeping the two thread strands together.	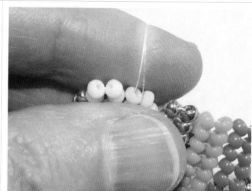
5. At the thread ends by your beadwork, make a loop of the two lengths of thread.	

6. Pull the loose ends through the loop.

7. Work the knot down to your work so it is right by the bead the thread is coming out of.

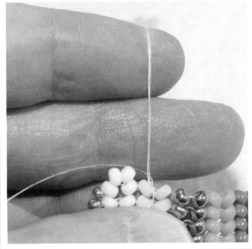

8. Pull the knot loop closed and make sure the knot is snug.

9. Put your needle on the two tail ends.
10. Run your needle DOWN through 4 beads of the column next to the bead where the thread is coming out.

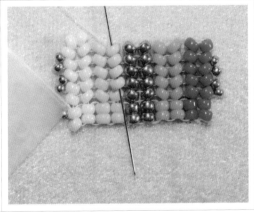

11. Run your needle UP through 4 beads of the column next to the bead where the thread is coming out.

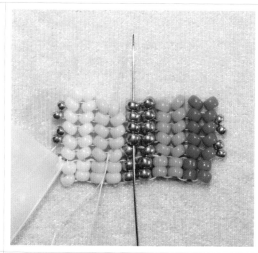

12. Run your needle DOWN through 4 beads of the column next to the bead where the thread is coming out.

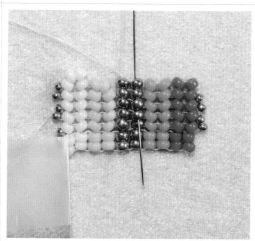

13. Run your needle UP through 4 beads of the column next to the bead where the thread is coming out.

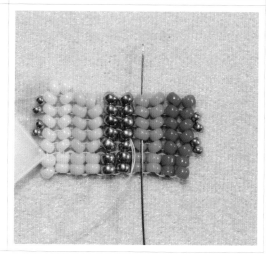

14. Trim the ends, making sure you do not cut the original threads below.

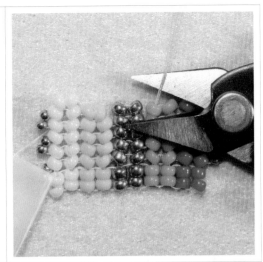

15. Put your needle on the long thread you added and continue adding beads to your work.

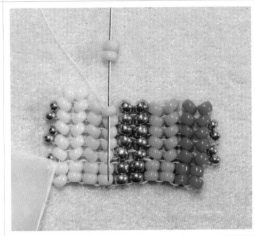

6 Add Your Clasp - Part 1

We are going to use a 5-strand slide clasp, which looks like this. The narrow end of the clasp slides into the wider end of the clasp when the bracelet is worn.

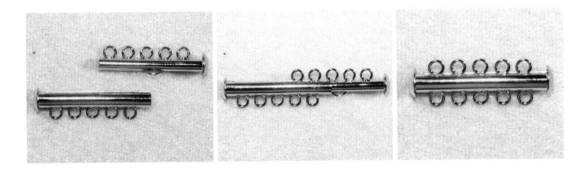

1. Slide your clasp pieces together.
2. Pick up one 8/0 bead and run your needle through the clasp, from back to front.

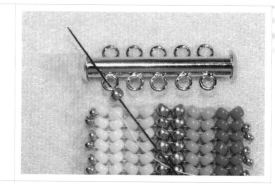

3. Run your needle DOWN through the bead you just added.

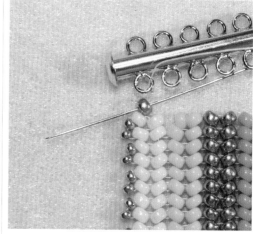

4. Run your needle DOWN through the next bead in line (the second bead in the row).

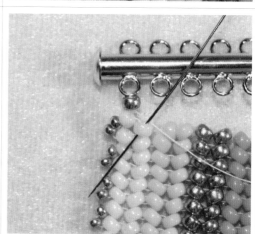

5. Run your needle UP through the next bead to the right of the bead where your thread is coming out.

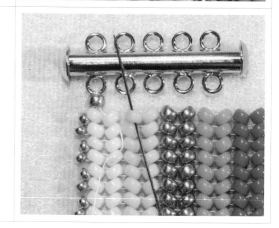

6. Pick up one 8/0 bead and run your needle through the clasp, from back to front.

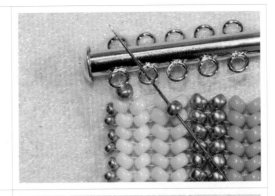

7. Run your needle DOWN through the bead you just added.

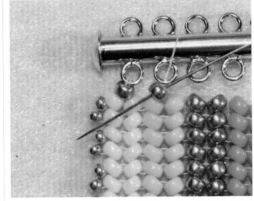

8. Run your needle DOWN through the next bead in line, the fourth bead in the row.

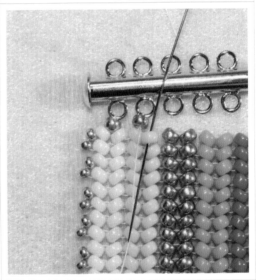

9. Repeat steps 5 through 8 until you have gone through all the loops on this side of the clasp.

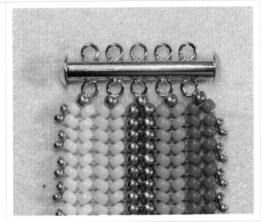

10. Run your needle under the thread bridge between the end bead of the first and second rows. This will allow us to turn around to reinforce the clasp.

11. Go UP through the end bead, the 8/0 connector bead and the loop.
12. Repeat the steps in this section until you have gone through all the loops and are where you started to add the clasp.
13. Run your needle down 10 columns and then back up 9 columns to secure your thread.
14. Trim your thread.

7 Add Your Clasp - Part 2

1. Remove the tape from your tail thread and put your needle on it.
2. Run your needle UP through the two 11/0 beads on the end where your tail thread is.

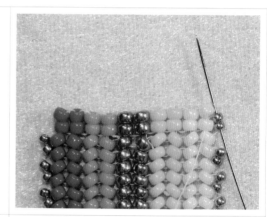

3. Run your needle UP through the first bead of the row.

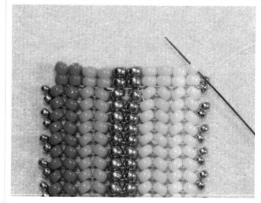

4. Bring the other end of the clasp to your work, making sure you don't twist the beadwork.
5. Pick up one 8/0 bead and go through the first loop on the end of the clasp.

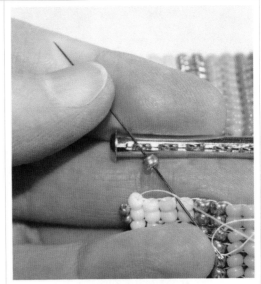

6. Run your needle DOWN through the bead you just added.

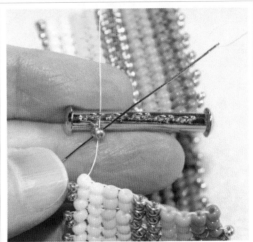

7. Run your needle DOWN through the next bead, the second bead of the row.

8. Run your needle UP through the bead next to the bead your thread is coming out of.
9. Repeat Steps 5 and 8 for the remaining loops of the clasp.

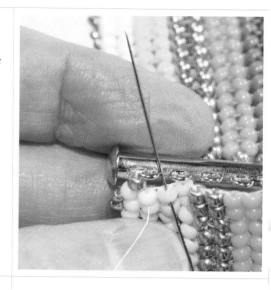

10. Run your thread back through the beads and loops, like you did on the first side.
11. Run your needle down 10 columns and then back up 9 columns to secure your thread.
12. Trim your thread.

13. Your bracelet is finished!

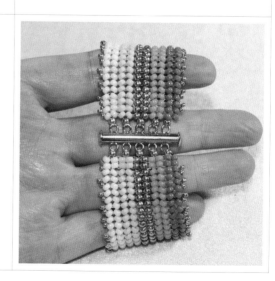

Congratulations! Your herringbone bracelet is finished!

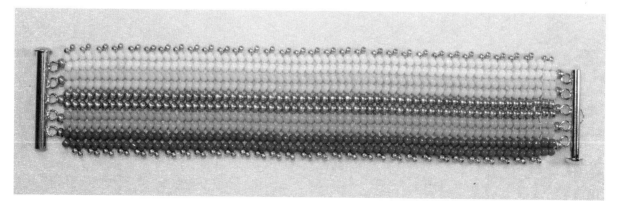

Made in the USA
Columbia, SC
30 November 2017